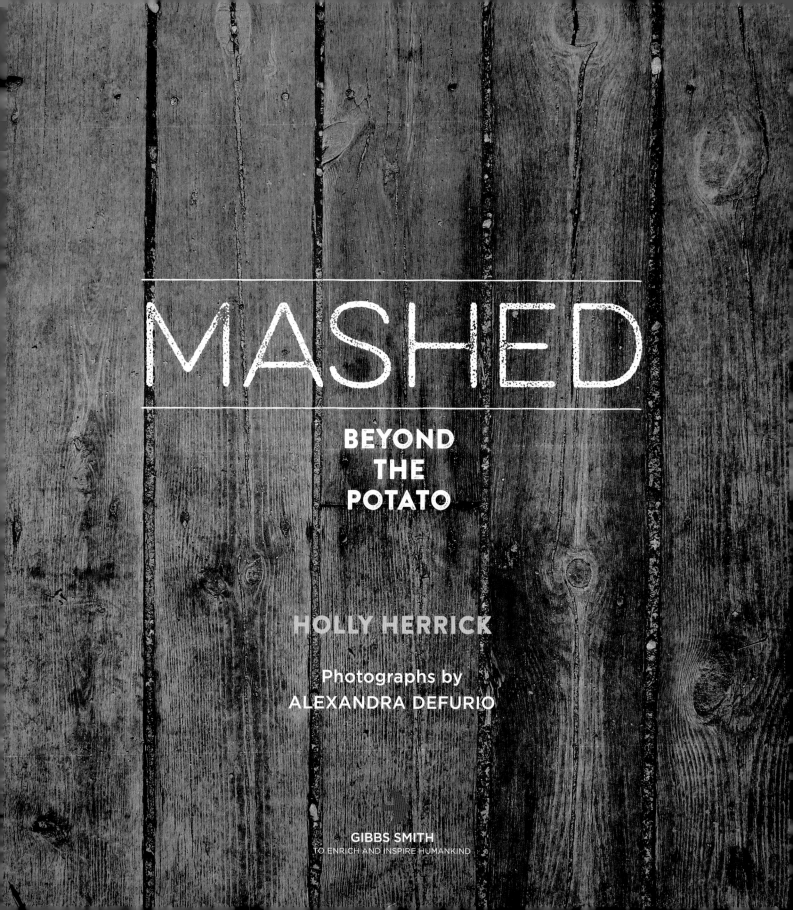

MASHED

BEYOND THE POTATO

HOLLY HERRICK

Photographs by
ALEXANDRA DEFURIO

GIBBS SMITH
TO ENRICH AND INSPIRE HUMANKIND

First Edition
20 19 18 17 16   5 4 3 2 1

Published by
Gibbs Smith
P.O. Box 667
Layton, Utah 84041

1.800.835.4993 orders
www.gibbs-smith.com

Designed by Rita Sowins / Sowins Design
Printed and bound in Hong Kong
Gibbs Smith books are printed on paper produced from sustainable PEFC-certified forest/controlled wood source. Learn more at www.pefc.org.

Library of Congress Cataloging-in-Publication Data

Names: Herrick, Holly, author.
Title: Mashed : beyond the potato / Holly Herrick.
Description: First Edition. | Layton, Utah : Gibbs Smith, 2016. | Includes index.
Identifiers: LCCN 2016003382 | ISBN 9781423644477 (hardcover)
Subjects: LCSH: Cooking, American. | Cooking (Soft foods) | LCGFT: Cookbooks.
Classification: LCC TX715 .H567 2016 | DDC 641.5973—dc23
LC record available at https://lccn.loc.gov/2016003382

To my darling Michael Keating
for daily inspirations on life and cooking and
patiently listening to me mutter on about
all things mashed for several months.

CONTENTS

INTRODUCTION

"That which is not good is not delicious to a well-governed and wise appetite."
—John Milton, 1608–1674, *Comus*

As celebrated poet John Milton so correctly points out, "That which is not good is not delicious." As a long-time restaurant critic, frequently subjected to eating bad food (as well as a whole lot of delicious food), and a dedicated chef, instructor, and eight-time cookbook author, I will add my personal motto to his thoughts: Life is too short to eat bad food, mashed or otherwise.

Indeed, mashed foods conjure up images of comfort, even childhood. During the process of writing this book, I kept envisioning a young child barely bellied up to a table in a chair that's too big and low, cradling an oversize spoon, eagerly digging into some mashed deliciousness, legs dangling, toes tapping in anticipation, butter dripping down his chin. Maybe it was a subliminal me? There is probably a little bit of that kid in all of us, which is a big reason why writing this book was so much fun for me, and hopefully will be equally fun for you to read and cook from.

In addition to comfort, mashed foods inspire the notion of simplicity, which is largely true. But, as I've learned going through life, particularly in cooking, making "simple" food delicious presents an extra challenge. What makes average mashed potatoes stand out from unforgettable, delicious ones, the kind you dream about? What makes a fruit compote sing, or a winter root vegetable mash make you want to sing?

As you work your way through this book, you'll see that the answers boil down to a few simple concepts that require dedication to reach ethereal, delicious mashed food levels. The most important thing is to start out with the freshest, best-quality food and ingredients you can find. You can't make delicious from tired or processed.

Second, consider the texture of the principal ingredient. Not unlike matching the right accessory with a dress, or the right place to hang a painting on the wall, you want to think about what might complement it. Barley in mashed potatoes? Probably not, but cauliflower? Absolutely, yes.

Layering flavors is also essential. The recipes throughout this book are designed to build upon inherent flavors in any given food and layer them back into the dish. For example, going back to cauliflower, the water or stock in which it is simmered is later brought back into the dish, avoiding waste (and throwing away nutrition) and doubling up on flavor. Many fruits and vegetables are roasted and then mashed, which is another way of doing the very same thing. Stocks, broths, wines, and other flavoring ingredients are reduced or steeped and then delicately returned to whence they came.

Finally, choosing the right method to mash (Basic Mashing Tools, page 10) is mandatory. It's like matching the right color makeup to your skin tone. The wrong one will make you look ill, while the right one is barely perceptible, perfectly beautiful and natural. For example, mashing potatoes with a food processor is equivalent to turning them to glue, while a food mill or old-fashioned manual masher will render the potatoes into fluffy spud pillows, eagerly awaiting the butter and cream they'll readily absorb to make them sublime.

Throughout the pages I strive to clearly define and make understandable some of these rules, but remember with rules, there are always exceptions. It is my hope you'll use the methods, inspirations, and concepts to create some memorable, always delicious, mashed treats using your palate and finesse as a personal guide.

As always, bon appétit!

HOLLY

BASIC MASHING TOOLS

MANUAL MASHER This is the stalwart of the mashed kitchen and can be used to mash almost anything, as long as it's got a little elbow grease behind it. Most come in one of two varieties, with a mash element that looks more like a grid or with a mash element that looks more like the coils on a furnace. I own the former, and find it works very well. Manual mashers work best with soft, pliable cooked vegetables or fruits and yield a more rustic effect, as in the Ultimate Mashed Potatoes Master Recipe—Rustic Version (page 17). To use it, just push down and through what you're working with, swirling a little to bring stray bits back into the bowl and into the mash fold.

FOOD MILL Another old-school manual-masher method, it remains one of the best, particularly for foods you want to cook with the skin on (such as tomatoes, apples, pears, or potatoes) for flavor and nutrition reasons, but ultimately want the skins removed in the mashing process. Food mills come with many different-size holes (also known as rice) and operate by turning the handle around the mill, going backward from time to time to further press the contents. The mill will hold the skins, but release the milled food through the bottom. Using one sets the stage for some of the fluffiest, most elegant mashed potatoes and applesauces imaginable.

FOOD PROCESSOR For the purposes of mashing, I almost always use mine fitted with a metal blade. A food processor is extra well-suited to puréeing more dense foods (like Brussels sprouts or celery root) or getting a very silky, smooth purée on roasted vegetables and some soups.

ELECTRIC BLENDER Though I use this less throughout the book, it's ideal for blending creams into compotes (such as the milk shake) or any time you want to build extra froth into your mash. It's not very well-suited to recipes containing a large ratio of hot liquid to solid, cooked matter. The liquid will often seep from the bottom.

IMMERSION BLENDERS The best friend of a lazy dishwasher and a sensible cook, these mash-friendly tools are named after their function. They are immersed into whatever they're going to mash, most often into a soup pot to purée the ingredients as much or as little as you like. A quick whir (as I call it), will break up the threads of tougher greens (such as collards), yielding a kind of mini mash, while a full-on purée will completely emulsify most foods. Sometimes larger or harder chunks of food need a little nudge to get started. I do this by running the blender, pressing directly down onto the harder pieces, and ultimately integrating the entire pot into a purée. Not only do they save washing additional pots, but they're also extremely easy to wash themselves, usually requiring only a little swish through hot, soapy water.

HAND-HELD ELECTRIC MIXER For the purposes of recipes in *Mashed*, this was used exclusively for mounting egg whites and whipped cream. A whisk can do the same thing, but it's a bit more work.

PREPARATION TIPS

CHIFFONADE This is a term used for slicing delicate herbs or lettuces into very thin strips. It is most easily accomplished by stacking the leaves of whatever you're using, such as fresh basil, in a manageable pile, roughly 8 leaves or so. These are then rolled, like a cigar, and chopped through with a sharp chef's knife to create thin $1/8$-inch-wide ribbons. This method prevents bruising or damaging the delicate greens.

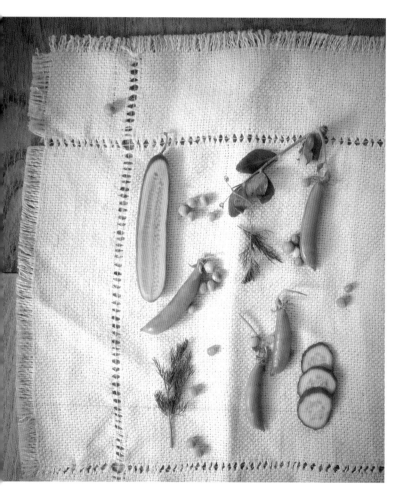

CELERY ROOT (CELERIAC) TIPS Once difficult to find, celery root is a mainstay in the produce section of most grocery markets, particularly during cooler months. Look for its distinctive knobby, pocked exterior and large, bulbous shape. It's not pretty, but it sure is delicious. Like rutabaga, it has a double skin: the thick outer skin, and an inner skin, usually about $1/4$ inch (6 mm) thick. To remove both, which is necessary, cut off the top of the root and position it bottom side down securely on your cutting surface. Using a sharp chef's knife, cut down and through the skins in broad swaths, as you would remove the rind from a melon. Keep turning until you're all the way through the root. Cut off any brown flecks or discolored areas, slice, and cook quickly. It will discolor if left exposed to oxygen more than a few minutes in its raw state.

AVOCADO TIPS There are several avocado varieties, but the smaller, thicker skinned dark-green Hass avocados have more concentrated texture and flavor than some of their counterparts and are most commonly available. All avocados are ripe when they yield slightly to pressure from your forefinger. They become darker green to almost black when they are very ripe, and will start to develop soft and discolored spots at this point. To accelerate ripening, place avocado in a paper bag with a ripe banana or another ripe fruit. To decelerate the ripening, refrigerate until ready to use. To remove the pit, once avocado is halved, tap hard with the cutting edge of a large knife and twist. It should pop right out.

HOW TO CLEAN A LEEK Because leeks grow up from the dirt and their layers are so tightly bound, they tend to harbor grit and dirt in surprise places and need to be cleaned very carefully. There are two ways to do it. In both cases, most of the tough green tops are cut off and discarded or saved for making stock. For lightly soiled leeks, cut an X about 1 inch deep into the top of the trimmed leek and run it under water, loosening the petals around the X to remove any grit. Extra-dirty leeks should be cut into thick slices after they're trimmed, and soaked in a bowl or sink of cold water; give good swish, rinse, and repeat until all of the grit is gone.

POMEGRANATE POWER Considered a superfood for its high nutrient content, pomegranate can be purchased in its whole form during the cooler months and, increasingly, already seeded or juiced. The seeds are called arils and they look like little rubies. Getting them out of their tightly knitted pockets can be a challenge, but it's worth the effort. An easy way to get to the fruit is to quarter the pomegranate, revealing the four cores, then peel back the bitter pith pockets and release the arils. One pomegranate will yield 1 to 2 cups (175 to 350 g) of arils.

AN EASY WAY TO DEVEIN SHRIMP Use a good set of kitchen shears and cut through the exterior, rounded edge of the shrimp from top to just above the tail. Cut right through the shell and about $1/8$ inch (3 mm) deep to expose the vein. Use your fingers or a paring knife to guide out the vein and discard. Carefully rinse the shrimp and shells. This works equally well for cooked and raw shrimp.

POTATOES

Of all things mashed, potatoes are likely the most universally known and adored. The kid in all of us can barely resist the thought of sitting down to a steaming bowl of creamy potato deliciousness, preferably with a melting pool of butter at the top, trickling like molten, golden love down a fluffy mashed potato mountain.

Because potatoes have such a neutral flavor (earthy, buttery, slightly nutty), they open up the door to a huge pantry of spice, herb, and ingredient pairings, from blue cheese to nuts, literally. Of course, all potatoes are not created equal, and some are better suited to particular preparations than others. There are hundreds of varieties grown around the world, and in the United States, there are more than 100 kinds available. Under this large potato umbrella (which includes red, white, yellow, purple/blue, fingerling, and petite potatoes), there are essentially three potato types:

WAXY These thin-skinned potatoes have a lower starch content and a higher moisture content. They hold their shape very well when cooked and are best used for roasting, boiling, casseroles, and potato salads. Popular varieties include red bliss and new potatoes.

IDAHO/RUSSET This celebrated baking potato has a much higher starch content and lower moisture content. Unlike its waxy cousins, it tends to fall apart when cooked (unless when baked with its skin on). It's an excellent choice for baking, frying, and mashing.

ALL-PURPOSE The lead player in this medium starch content potato pool is the ubiquitous and delicious Yukon Gold. It's my favorite pick for mashed potatoes, but is also fabulous baked, fried, or in casseroles, salads, or gratins.

Many of these beautiful spuds are put to work in this chapter, as well as the popular sweet potato, which is so juicy hot right out of the oven that it begs for almost nothing except a dab of butter and a dusting of salt and pepper.

Before we get started, there are a few things to keep in mind about potatoes. All store best in cool, dark places (like a pantry or a cellar). Refrigerating raw potatoes will convert their starch to sugar and muddle both taste and texture. Many potatoes will discolor or oxidize once peeled and cut, so try to avoid doing so until just before cooking.

ULTIMATE MASHED POTATOES MASTER RECIPE–RUSTIC VERSION

YIELDS 6 SERVINGS

Making the ultimate bowl of mashed potatoes is not hard, but taking a few carefully calculated and timed steps will make all the difference between ho-hum and magnificent. It all begins with the potato. Yukon Gold is the best at absorbing just the right amount of liquid and seasoning while allowing pure potato flavor to shine through; russets will work, but I feel like their starchiness pulls in too much cream. Boiled potatoes should always start in cold, salted water. Once cooked, the potatoes need to be well-drained and returned to the pot to dry out over medium heat before receiving the cream/liquid. The cream and butter that are incorporated into the hot potatoes also need to be hot. They can be heated in a measuring cup in the microwave (high for 1–2 minutes) or simmered on the stove.

Keeping potatoes warm is as simple as setting a bowl of mashed potatoes over a water bath simmering gently over the stove—and don't be afraid to add additional hot cream as liquid potentially evaporates. Serve hot and well-seasoned.

6 medium to large Yukon Gold
  potatoes, peeled and cut into
  1½-inch (3.8-cm) cubes (about
  6 cups / 1.08 kg)
Water
2 tablespoons kosher or sea salt
1 cup (240 ml) half-and-half
3 tablespoons unsalted butter
½ cup sour cream, room
  temperature
1½ teaspoons kosher or sea salt
1 teaspoon ground black pepper

Place the potatoes into a medium pot and add enough cold water to cover generously. Add 2 tablespoons salt. Bring to a boil over high heat, reduce to a simmer, and cook, uncovered, until the potatoes are very tender and break apart with light pressure from a fork. Drain very well in a colander. Return potatoes to the same pot and dry out for 1–2 minutes, stirring, over medium heat.

Meanwhile, heat together the half-and-half and butter in a small skillet over medium heat until simmering (or in the microwave for 1–2 minutes on high heat). Using a standard manual masher (Basic Mashing Tools, page 10), begin breaking up the potatoes. Simultaneously, add the hot cream and butter in thirds. Once the cream is fully incorporated, mash in the sour cream, salt, and pepper. Taste and adjust seasonings as needed. Serve immediately or keep warm over a warm water bath (up to 1 hour), adding more cream as needed.

ULTIMATE MASHED POTATOES
MASTER RECIPE—ELEGANT VERSION

YIELDS 6 SERVINGS

This is exactly the same recipe as the Rustic Version (page 17), the only difference is you have the opportunity to save a step and leave the scrubbed skins on the Yukon Golds and pass them through a food mill (Basic Mashing Tools, page 10) before folding in the warm cream and butter. The resulting mashed potatoes are slightly more airy, and also smoother—decidedly more elegant. And the process of pressing the skins out of the potatoes, which are retained inside the food mill, provides another level of potato flavor and nutrition.

SUGGESTED VARIATIONS

FRESH HERBS Depending on what you're serving them with, mashed potatoes are a wonderful backdrop to many fresh herbs. Remember to add the fragile fine herbs (basil, tarragon, or chives) just before serving or they will wilt and discolor. Adding 3 tablespoons of finely chopped fresh rosemary to the master recipe goes beautifully with pork or chicken, or the same quantity of chives marries fantastically with sautéed sole or another delicate fish. Basil, cut into a fine chiffonade (page 12), is smashing with an Italian- or Thai-inspired side, while parsley adds a fresh smattering of earthy, green complementary flavor to almost anything.

GARLIC Sauté 6 cloves of thinly sliced garlic in 1 tablespoon of olive oil over medium-low heat until lightly caramelized and softened, 5–7 minutes. Smash the garlic with your chef's knife and fold into the master recipe—divinity! The flavors will develop further with a little heat, so keep it in the bowl over the water bath for a few minutes before serving.

HORSERADISH Whip 1 tablespoon of prepared horseradish into the master recipe, and you have a winning formula for a two-in-one-punch side and sauce for prime rib or anywhere horseradish is at home, including poached or grilled salmon.

TRUFFLE OIL/FRESH TRUFFLES The French and Italians have long recognized the beauty of mashed potatoes with this fragrant earthly delight. It's tough to find the real deal, but if you can find a beautiful fresh truffle (white or black), chop it up very finely and add a tablespoon or two to the master recipe. Alternatively, drizzle a generous teaspoon or so of best-quality truffle oil over warm mashed potatoes for an extra sexy, elegant finish.

BASIC RICED POTATOES

YIELDS ABOUT 4 CUPS (840 G)

Riced potatoes are actually baked potato flesh removed from the skins (save these) that are passed through a food mill. The resulting unadulterated potatoes are as light as air. Their fluffy texture is well-suited to many dishes. When you're making them, prepare several at once to save time and minimize waste. Any leftovers will freeze well, and you can get a nice batch of delicious potato skins (Cheddar-Bacon-Celery Skins, page 54) out of the deal. The same exact process can be used for sweet potatoes, which also have lovely texture when roasted (Sweet Potato Indian Pudding, page 62) though more moist and heavier.

8 medium russet potatoes, well-scrubbed and each pierced twice

Preheat oven to 425° F (220° C). Place the potatoes on the center rack and bake until the skins are bubbly and crisp, and they're tender all the way to the center when pierced with a knife. Remove from oven to cool.

When cool enough to handle, cut in half vertically and scoop out the cooked flesh with a soup spoon, being careful not to break or damage the skins. Reserve the skins separately. Process the cooked potato by passing through a food mill (Basic Mashing Tools, page 10) into a large bowl. Cover and refrigerate, or freeze up to few months. Use as directed in accompanying recipes.

DOUBLE-ONION MASHED WHAMMY

YIELDS 6 TO 8 SERVINGS

The delicate, subtle onion flavor of leeks goes beautifully with the sweetness and surprise color of red onions in this rustic green- and purple-flecked mash. Pair it with something equally rustic, such as meatloaf with pan gravy, or pot roast.

3 large Yukon Gold potatoes, peeled and cut into 1$\frac{1}{2}$-inch (3.8-cm) cubes (about 2$\frac{1}{2}$ cups / 450 g)

$\frac{1}{2}$ large red onion, peeled and cut into 1-inch (2.5-cm) cubes, about 1 cup (150 g)

2 leeks, base trimmed and dark-green leaves removed, cut into 1-inch (2.5-cm) dice and rinsed well in fresh cold water to remove grit

Water

2 tablespoons kosher or sea salt

1 cup (240 ml) half-and-half

3 tablespoons unsalted butter

1$\frac{3}{4}$ teaspoons kosher or sea salt

1 teaspoon ground black pepper

3 tablespoons finely chopped fresh parsley

Place the potatoes, red onion, and leeks in a medium pot. Add enough cold water to generously cover, along with 2 tablespoons salt. Bring to a boil over high heat and reduce to simmer. Cook, uncovered, until all of the ingredients are very tender, 20–25 minutes. Drain very well in a colander. Return to same pot and heat over medium heat for 1–2 minutes, stirring, to dry out the ingredients.

Meanwhile, heat the half-and-half and butter together in a small pan over medium heat (or in a microwave for 1–3 minutes on high heat), until heated through. Using a traditional manual masher (Basic Mashing Tools, page 10), begin breaking up the potato mixture. Add the hot cream and butter in thirds, mashing all along the way, until consistency is smooth. Add salt, pepper, and fresh parsley. Serve immediately or keep warm over simmering water bath.

GOLDEN CAULIFLOWER MASH

YIELDS 6 TO 8 SERVINGS

Yukon Golds provide much-needed texture levity to puréed cauliflower, while cauliflower provides snow-white color appeal and a smooth, buttery flavor that makes this mash an instant favorite. Processing with a food mill aerates and integrates the ingredients best of all, but a traditional manual masher will also work. A flurry of fresh chives at the end adds a beautiful touch. This makes the perfect side to complete a homey roasted chicken dinner.

5 medium Yukon Gold potatoes, peeled and cut into 1 1/2-inch (3.8-cm) cubes, about 5 cups (900 g)

1/2 head cauliflower, center stalk and base removed (about 2 cups / 460 g florets)

Water

2 tablespoons kosher or sea salt

1 cup (240 ml) half-and-half

3 tablespoons unsalted butter

1/2 cup (120 ml) sour cream

1 1/2 teaspoons kosher or sea salt

1 teaspoon ground black pepper

2 tablespoons finely chopped fresh chives

Place the potatoes and cauliflower in a medium pot. Add enough cold water to generously cover, along with 2 tablespoons salt. Bring to a boil over high heat and reduce to simmer. Cook, uncovered, until all of the ingredients are very tender, 20–25 minutes. Drain very well in a colander. Return to same pot and heat over medium heat for 1–2 minutes, stirring, to dry out the ingredients.

Meanwhile, heat the half-and-half and butter together in a small pan over medium heat (or in a microwave for 1–2 minutes on high heat), until heated through. Pour the cooked potatoes and cauliflower into the bowl of a food mill (Basic Mashing Tools, page 10), in batches (probably 3 depending on size of the food mill), positioned over a large bowl. Using a wooden spoon, stir in the hot half-and-half and butter in thirds. To finish, stir in the sour cream, salt, pepper, and fresh chives. Taste and adjust seasoning as necessary. Serve immediately or keep warm over simmering water bath.

COLOSSAL GREEK SHEPHERD'S PIE

YIELDS 8 TO 10 SERVINGS

Ground lamb, oregano, lemon, mint, artichokes, kalamata olives, and tangy feta cheese cast a lovely Greek glow on the leftover mashed potato base in this easily assembled dish that is perfect for entertaining guests and family alike. While this dish is toothsome and hearty, the sunny flavors of the Mediterranean keep it fresh and light. Use Ultimate Mashed Potatoes leftovers, either Rustic (page 17) or Elegant (page 18), if you have them. Otherwise, you'll need to make a fresh batch.

MEAT LAYER

1 tablespoon olive oil

1 pound (450 g) ground lamb

1/2 teaspoon kosher or sea salt

1/2 teaspoon ground black pepper

1 teaspoon dried oregano leaves

2 tablespoons fresh mint leaves, cut thinly into 1/8-inch (3-mm) ribbons (chiffonade, page 12)

1 tablespoon fresh lemon juice

1/4 cup (40 g) currants, optional

POTATO AND VEGETABLE LAYERS

3/4 cup (110 g) crumbled feta or goat cheese

3/4 cup (135 g) coarsely chopped pitted kalamata olives

3 cups (650 g) leftover mashed potatoes

1 cup (170 g) canned marinated artichoke hearts, drained, rinsed, and coarsely chopped

TOPPING

1/3 cup (40 g) ricotta cheese

Preheat oven to 375° F (190° C). Begin with the meat layer. Heat the olive oil in a large skillet over medium high. Crumble in the lamb, salt, and pepper. Cook, stirring and breaking up with a wooden spoon, until browned, about 8 minutes. Drain off any excess fat and discard. Stir in the oregano, mint, lemon juice, and currants. Taste and adjust seasonings as needed.

To compile, using a paper towel, rub down the interior bottom and sides of a large casserole pan with olive oil. Stir the feta and kalamata olives into the mashed potatoes until combined. Using a spatula, evenly arrange the potato mixture in a single layer in the bottom of the casserole pan. Top this with an even layer of artichokes. Top this with the reserved meat mixture, spreading evenly.

To finish, place small dollops of ricotta cheese on top of the meat mixture, pressing down to spread into the meat. Bake, uncovered, for 40 minutes, or until bubbling and hot. Let set for 10 minutes before serving. Serve hot with a simple garden salad.

TRADITIONAL ENGLISH SHEPHERD'S PIE

YIELDS 8 TO 10 SERVINGS

This recipe uses leftover potatoes from the Ultimate Mashed Potatoes Master Recipes (page 17 or page 18). If you are missing leftovers, you'll need to prepare a fresh batch. Other purée bases that are well-suited to this dish include Triple-Threat Celery Mash (page 43), Purely Parsnip Purée (page 98), and Buttery Parsley Rutabaga Mash (page 90). This recipe is good enough to put any of them to fresh use. A thick layer of bubbly mild cheddar tops it all off.

MEAT LAYER

1 tablespoon unsalted butter

1/2 cup (120 g) finely chopped red onion or shallot

1 1/4 pounds (570 g) 80 percent lean/20 percent fat ground beef

1 teaspoon kosher or sea salt

1/2 teaspoon ground black pepper

1 teaspoon ground curry powder (red, yellow, or green)

POTATO AND VEGETABLE LAYERS

3 cups (650 g) leftover mashed potatoes

2 tablespoons unsalted butter

3 medium carrots, peeled and cut into 1/4-inch (6-mm) dice (about 1 1/2 cups / 190 g)

Pinch of kosher or sea salt and ground black pepper

2 tablespoons water

1 1/2 cups (200 g) frozen sweet peas

1/4 cup (10 g) finely chopped fresh parsley

2 tablespoons butter, room temperature

3 cups (360 g) grated mild or medium cheddar cheese

MEAT LAYER Preheat oven to 350° F (175° C). Melt butter in a large sauté pan over medium heat. Add the onion and cook, stirring until softened, about 5 minutes. Crumble in the beef and season with salt and pepper. Stir to break up the beef, and brown over medium heat, 5–8 minutes. Drain off all visible fat and discard. Reserve beef in the pan and stir in curry powder.

POTATO AND VEGETABLE LAYERS Prepare and reserve the mashed potatoes separately. Melt butter in a large skillet over medium heat. Add the carrots, salt, and pepper. Toss to evenly coat in butter and seasoning. Add the water, reduce the heat to medium low and cook, uncovered, until the water has cooked off and the carrots have softened al dente, about 5 minutes. Stir in the peas and parsley and remove from the heat. Set aside.

To compile, butter the bottom and sides of a large casserole pan with the room-temperature butter. Add the prepared beef mixture, spreading evenly with a spatula. Add the pea-and-carrot mixture, spreading evenly with a spatula. Finish with the potatoes, spreading evenly. Top with an even layer of the cheese. Bake, uncovered, until bubbly and heated through, 40–45 minutes. Let set for 10 minutes before cutting. Serve hot.

ELEGANT SMASHED EGG AND SWEET GHERKIN POTATO SALAD

YIELDS 8 TO 10 SERVINGS

Finely puréed hard-boiled eggs, barely bound with sour cream and mayonnaise, get a sweet, pungent bite from tiny bites of chopped sweet gherkin pickles in this refined, waxy red potato salad. The simplicity of this salad is what makes it so perfect.

EGGS
4 large eggs, room temperature
Water
1 tablespoon vinegar

SALAD
10 medium (about 2 pounds / 900 g) unpeeled waxy red potatoes, well-scrubbed and cut into 1-inch (2.5-cm) cubes
Water
1 tablespoon kosher or sea salt
1 cup (230 g) full-fat sour cream
$1/2$ cup (120 g) mayonnaise
1 tablespoon Dijon mustard
6 sweet gherkin pickles, very finely chopped (about $1/2$ cup / 80 g)
3 tablespoons sweet gherkin pickle juice (from the jar)
2 teaspoons kosher or sea salt
1 teaspoon ground black pepper
3 scallions, base and green tops trimmed to 3 inches (7.6 cm) above white base, very finely chopped on the bias

For the eggs, gently place the eggs in a medium pot. Cover generously with water (at least 2 inches / 5 cm above the eggs) and add vinegar. Bring to a boil over high heat. Once at a full boil, remove from heat and keep the eggs in the heated water for exactly 15 minutes. Drain. Place the eggs in a bowl of heavily iced cold water for exactly 5 minutes. Drain.

Peel and remove the shell of each egg under running tap water. Cut the eggs in half and process the whites and yolks in the bowl of a food processor or through a food mill (Basic Mashing Tools, page 10) until flour fine then turn out into a large bowl. Set aside.

To finish the salad, place the potatoes in a medium pot, cover with cold water, add salt, and bring to a boil over high heat. Reduce heat to medium low and cook, uncovered, for 15–18 minutes until very tender, but still holding their shape. Drain well and cool.

Return to the reserved eggs and whisk in the sour cream, mayonnaise, mustard, gherkins, and pickle juice until smooth. Stir in the salt, pepper, and scallions. Gently fold in the reserved potatoes and stir to combine. Cover with plastic wrap and refrigerate for 1 hour (and up to overnight) to allow the flavors to develop.

Remove from the refrigerator at least 15 minutes before serving to bring the salad closer to room temperature, where it will have its fullest flavor. It's beautiful and delicious beside a small mound of arugula or served in tender lettuce (such as Bibb or Boston) cups.

BLUE CHEESE AND BLACK PEPPER DUCHESSE POTATOES

YIELDS 8 SERVINGS

No blue cheese and peppercorn sauce required for your fillet, not with this gutsy potato sharing the same plate. The sweetness of a gentle blue cheese hits just the right note with the heat of black pepper. Both are tempered by a bit of cream and butter, which flesh out these twice-baked beauties. Because the potatoes can be fully prepped ahead of time and baked just before serving, they are excellent menu picks for entertaining.

4 medium russet potatoes (about 3/4 pound / 340 g each), well-scrubbed and pierced 3 times with a knife

3/4 cup (180 ml) half-and-half

2 tablespoons unsalted butter, room temperature

2/3 cup (90 g) crumbled mild blue cheese

1/2 teaspoon kosher or sea salt

1 teaspoon ground black pepper

1 tablespoon finely chopped fresh parsley

Preheat oven to 425° F (220° C). Place potatoes on a baking sheet. Bake until the jackets start to crisp and the centers are extremely tender when pierced with a knife, about 1 hour (more for a larger potato). Remove from oven and reserve until cool enough to handle.

Cut each potato in half vertically. Gently scoop out the filling of each half, leaving approximately 1/4-inch (6-mm) border of cooked flesh on each potato, being careful not to break through the skin. If necessary, cut a small flat space on the bottom center of each half so it can sit upright when returned to baking sheet for second cooking.

Place the scooped potato flesh into a large bowl. Mash, using a manual masher, or for a fluffier finish, blend with an electric mixer (Basic Mashing Tools, page 10), with half-and-half, butter, and blue cheese. Add the salt and pepper and taste to adjust seasoning as needed. Gently spoon the filling back into the reserved potato halves, forming a small mound on top of each.

Place the filled potatoes on a rimmed baking sheet and return to preheated 425° F (220° C) oven. Cook for 25–30 minutes, until puffy, hot, and just golden on top. Serve hot, with a light crumbling of blue cheese, freshly ground black pepper, and a sprinkle of fresh parsley. Crunchy, smoky grilled steaks are a welcome addition to this side party!

RICOTTA, LEMON, AND BASIL POTATO CAKES

YIELDS 8 LARGE SERVINGS

Mashed potatoes have a way of disappearing quickly in my home. They probably do in yours, too. On the rare occasion I do have some leftover mashed goodness hanging around, one of the best ways to repurpose them is to mold them into crispy fried potato cakes. The lightness of ricotta turns these cakes into veritable potato cloud puffs, threaded with lemon zest and fresh basil, with a crunchy panko bread crumb exterior. The Japanese crumbs, available in most groceries these days, give an extra enticing crispy edge to the cakes—if you can't find them, substitute unseasoned traditional bread crumbs.

3 cups (650 g) leftover or freshly prepared mashed potatoes (Ultimate Mashed Potatoes Master Recipes, page 17 or page 18)

½ cup (55 g) sifted all-purpose flour

1 egg yolk, beaten

¼ to ½ cup (30 to 60 g) full-fat ricotta cheese (depends on wetness of the mashed potatoes)

2 tablespoons fresh basil, cut into chiffonade (page 12)

Zest of 1 lemon

3 cups (360 g) panko bread crumbs

½ cup (120 ml) vegetable oil

1 tablespoon unsalted butter

Kosher or sea salt and freshly ground pepper, to taste

Stir together mashed potatoes, flour, egg yolk, ricotta, basil, and lemon zest in a large bowl, combining thoroughly using a wooden spoon. Arrange the panko in a shallow pan or bowl. Using either your own clean hands or a ½-cup (120-ml) ice cream scoop, drop the mashed mixture into the panko crumbs and roll until the potatoes are covered well. Ensure that the crumbs are fully embedded to form a double-layer crust. Using your palms, press the cakes down into even round disks and arrange on a baking sheet. Repeat until all of the cakes have been formed (about 8 cakes). Chill in refrigerator, covered, for at least 30 minutes (and up to 24 hours) before frying.

Heat the oil and butter in a large nonstick skillet over medium-high heat until just sizzling. Add 4 of the prepped cakes to the pan in a single layer with ample space (a good ½ inch / 13 mm) between each cake. Lightly season the top of each with salt and pepper. Reduce heat to medium and cook the cakes until golden, about 4 minutes. Flip each cake, being careful not to splatter the oil or tear the cakes. Repeat cooking on the second side until golden, only 3 minutes this side. Remove with a slotted spatula and drain on a paper towel–lined tray. Season lightly. Repeat frying process with the second batch. Serve immediately, or reserve in a warm (200° F / 95° C) oven up to 30 minutes before serving. Garnish with fresh basil leaves and a lemon slice.

TWO POTATO AND HAM CHOWDER WITH FRESH THYME

YIELDS 8 TO 10 SERVINGS

Starchy-turned-silky russet potatoes merge with traditional aromatic leek, onion, garlic, and celery soup bedfellows; purée with cream and simmer again with colorful chunks of waxy red potatoes and smoked ham bites to finish this luscious soup. A smattering of fresh thyme announces a delicate lemony finish. If fatback is not easily found where you live, substitute a few tablespoons of rendered bacon fat to get things started. Save the crisped bacon to crumble over the finished soup before serving.

4 ($\frac{1}{2}$-inch / 13-mm) wide strips fatback, well-rinsed of additional exterior salt

2 tablespoons unsalted butter

2 leeks, well-rinsed white base only, trimmed and cut into $\frac{1}{2}$-inch (13-mm) dice (about 2 cups / 180 g)

1 medium onion, cut into medium dice (about $\frac{3}{4}$ cup / 113 g)

3 cloves garlic, smashed and coarsely chopped

1 large stalk celery, cleaned and cut into coarse $\frac{1}{2}$-inch (13-mm) dice (about 2 cups / 200 g)

2 teaspoons kosher or sea salt, divided

1$\frac{1}{2}$ teaspoons ground black pepper, divided

5 to 6 small to medium russet potatoes, peeled and cut into 1-inch (2.5-cm) dice (about 4 cups / 720 g)

1 to 2 tablespoons sweet vermouth

4 cups (960 ml) low-sodium chicken stock

$\frac{1}{2}$ pound (230 g) boneless smoked ham steak, cut into $\frac{1}{4}$-inch (6-mm) dice (about 2$\frac{1}{2}$ cups / 450 g)

2 medium waxy red potatoes, unpeeled and well-scrubbed, cut into $\frac{1}{4}$-inch (6-mm) dice (about 2 cups / 360 g)

2 tablespoons finely chopped fresh thyme

1 cup (240 ml) half-and-half

1 cup (240 ml) whole milk

2 tablespoons unsalted butter

Heat a 5$\frac{1}{2}$-quart (5-l) heavy-bottom pot over medium heat. Add fatback and butter and heat together until butter is melted. Add leeks, onion, garlic, celery, 1 teaspoon salt, and $\frac{1}{2}$ teaspoon pepper. Stir to coat. Continue cooking over medium heat until the vegetables have softened, about 5 minutes. Add the russet potatoes, vermouth, and chicken stock. Bring to a boil over high heat, reduce to a simmer over medium-low heat, and cook, uncovered, for 20 minutes, or until the potatoes are very tender and falling apart. Remove fatback and discard.

continued>

Using an immersion blender (Basic Mashing Tools, page 10) or traditional blender, purée until very smooth. For a chunkier, more rustic version, a thorough mash with a manual masher (Basic Mashing Tools, page 10) is also an excellent option. In the same pot, add the ham, red potatoes, thyme, half-and-half, milk, remaining salt, and remaining pepper. Bring to a boil over high heat and reduce to medium low, cooking uncovered, stirring occasionally, until the red potatoes are very tender, about 20 minutes.

Add butter just before serving and stir through until melted. Serve hot with fresh thyme sprigs for garnish. The soup stores very well covered and refrigerated for up to 3 days. Add extra cream or milk, as needed, to reheat.

SALMON AND CHIVE MASHED POTATOES

YIELDS 8 SERVINGS

Pink flecks of canned salmon and green spots of fresh chives wink fresh spring spunk and flavor into this beautiful bowl of spuds.

1 full recipe Ultimate Mashed
Potatoes Master Recipe—Rustic
Version (page 17)
1 (5-ounce / 140-g) can boneless
pink salmon, drained
¼ cup (10 g) finely chopped fresh
chives

Prepare the mashed potatoes as per directions. Mash in the salmon with a manual masher (Basic Mashing Tools, page 10). Fold in the chives. Serve hot. These potatoes are delicious as a meal with a green salad on the side.

SMASHED GOUDA AND ROSEMARY CRUSTED BABY YELLOW POTATOES

YIELDS 4 TO 6 SERVINGS

The thin skins of these waxy, slightly sweet, dense potatoes (you can substitute red or white varieties), pop with a gentle smash from the masher after they are braised to tenderness in stock. Browning in butter on both sides before drizzling with fresh rosemary and smoky Gouda cheese for a quick, bubbly broil add an inviting crunch factor and gooey cheese to every bite. Reminiscent of particularly indulgent potato skins, they are lovely with pork chops or roasted chicken.

18 to 20 baby yellow potatoes, 1 to 2 inches (2.5 to 5 cm) thick, scrubbed and pierced once with a knife

2 cups (480 ml) chicken stock

2 sprigs fresh rosemary

1/4 teaspoon kosher or sea salt

4 tablespoons unsalted butter, divided

1/2 cup (120 ml) water

1 tablespoon finely chopped fresh rosemary

1 cup (60 g) grated smoked Gouda cheese or sharp cheddar

1/2 teaspoon ground black pepper

Sour cream

Cut any of the potatoes that are noticeably larger than the others down to a roughly equivalent size. Arrange the potatoes in a single layer in a large ovenproof sauté pan. Pour in the chicken stock, adding just enough to cover halfway. Tuck the rosemary sprigs into the liquid and add salt. Bring to a boil over high, reduce to simmer over low, and cover, cooking for 10 minutes. Turn the potatoes over, cover, and cook on low for another 10 minutes, or until very tender. Remove cover and discard rosemary sprigs. Increase heat to high and cook off any remaining stock, uncovered, about 10 minutes.

Meanwhile, preheat broiler to high. When the liquid in the potato pan is down to a glaze, add 2 tablespoons butter. Swish to melt and reach the bottoms of all the potatoes. Reduce heat to medium, add remaining butter, swishing to coat, and leave untouched for 4 minutes, until potatoes are caramelized and golden on the bottom. Turn each potato over and smash individually, pressing down gently with a manual masher (Basic Mashing Tools, page 10) until they flatten to about 1/2 inch (13 mm) thick and pop. Add water to deglaze pan. Sprinkle the top of the potatoes with rosemary, cheese, and pepper. Broil for 3–5 minutes until bubbly and golden. Serve immediately with a dollop of sour cream on each serving, if desired.

TRIPLE-THREAT CELERY MASH

YIELDS 8 SERVINGS

When living in France decades ago, I discovered celery root, or celeriac, which is the bulb that yields the stalks that yield the leaves, all of which have wonderfully distinct and varied levels of celery flavor. The crunch and the freshness of the stalks, the fluttery light aroma of the leaves, and the layered buttery celery essence of the root all come together in one place in this magnificent dish. Its gamy vegetable flavor would work magic with roasted rabbit, duck, goose, or venison—making it an almost automatic annual holiday table showstopper!

1 large celery root, rough outer skin and inner skin removed and discarded (page 12), cut into 1-inch (2.5-cm) cubes (about 4 cups / 400 g)

2 medium russet potatoes, peeled and cut into 1-inch (2.5-cm) cubes (about 2 cups / 360 g)

2 stalks celery, trimmed, cleaned, and cut into 1-inch (2.5-cm) lengths

Water

1 tablespoon kosher or sea salt

1 cup (240 ml) heavy cream

3 tablespoons butter

1 teaspoon celery seed

2 tablespoons unsalted butter

1 teaspoon kosher or sea salt

1/2 teaspoon ground black pepper

Finely chopped celery leaves

Place the celery root, potatoes, and celery in a medium pot. Cover generously with cold water. Add 1 tablespoon salt. Bring to a boil over high and reduce to a simmer over medium-low heat. Cook, uncovered, for 30 minutes, or until all ingredients are very tender when pierced with a knife. Drain thoroughly in a colander and return to the warm cooking pot. Heat the celery mixture over medium heat for 1–2 minutes, shaking to move around the pan and dry out the ingredients.

Heat the cream, butter, and celery seed in a saucepan or in the microwave until warm and melted. Pour into the celery mixture, in thirds, mashing coarsely with a manual masher (Basic Mashing Tools, page 10) to combine and purée. Season with salt and pepper, tasting to adjust as needed. Serve hot, and garnish with a few chopped celery leaves. The mash will store beautifully in a sealed container in the refrigerator for up to 3 days. Reheat over a water bath or in the microwave.

SMASHED BABY RED POTATOES WITH GARLIC AND CHIVES

YIELDS 4 TO 6 SERVINGS

These plucky little red potatoes are always at the ready in my pantry. They do almost all the work as they simmer their way to tender along with a few cloves of garlic. The finish in this recipe is fast and simple: a manual mash with lots of butter, a dash of cream, salt, pepper, and a flurry of pungent fresh green chives. It's the perfect side for roasted chicken, burgers, or a steak. They reheat just as easily in the microwave (though it will alter the texture just slightly) as they do over a water bath.

About 24 (2 cups / 360 g) unpeeled and scrubbed baby red potatoes*

4 large cloves garlic, peeled and smashed

1 tablespoon kosher or sea salt

Water

1 cup (240 ml) half-and-half

4 tablespoons unsalted butter

1 teaspoon kosher or sea salt

1 teaspoon ground black pepper

1/4 cup (13 g) finely chopped fresh chives

Place the potatoes in a medium pot with garlic, 1 tablespoon salt, and enough water to cover. Bring to a boil over high heat, uncovered, and reduce to a simmer over medium low. Cook until the potatoes are very tender when pierced with a knife, about 25 minutes. Drain well in a colander.

Heat together the half-and-half and butter in a saucepan or in the microwave until melted and warm. Return the potatoes to the cooking pot. Drizzle in the warmed cream and butter, mashing with a manual masher (Basic Mashing Tools, page 10). You're shooting for a fat, chunky texture. A few mashes and swirls will do. Add the salt and pepper and combine. Gently fold in the fresh chives just before serving. Taste and adjust seasoning as needed. Serve steaming hot.

*The potatoes will be about the diameter of a quarter. Cut any that are noticeably larger so that all are about the same size and will cook evenly.

CAULIFLOWER MASHED POTATOES

YIELDS 6 SERVINGS

Cauliflower practically melts into the reduced quantity of potatoes in this delicate mash, fooling even the most practiced palate into believing they're eating 100 percent potatoes. Great for lower carb and calorie dining, this fluffy, aerated mash also takes less cream due to the higher moisture content of the cauliflower. Serve with salmon or another mild fish, like cod or flounder, and a mound of lightly dressed greens.

1 head cauliflower, quartered, cored, and cut into medium florets (about 6 cups / 1.375 kg)

2 large russet potatoes, peeled and cut into 2-inch (5-cm) chunks

1 tablespoon kosher or sea salt

Water

3/4 to 1 cup (180 to 240 ml) half-and-half, warmed

3 tablespoons unsalted butter

1 teaspoon kosher or sea salt

1/2 teaspoon ground black pepper

Place the cauliflower, potatoes, and salt in a large pot with just enough cold water to cover. Bring to a boil over high heat, reduce to a simmer over medium-low heat, and cook, uncovered, until tender, about 20 minutes. Drain well in a colander.

Return the mixture to the cooking pot, stream in the half-and-half, and mash with a manual masher (Basic Mashing Tools, page 10) until chunky smooth. Stir in the butter, salt, and pepper. Taste and adjust seasoning as needed. Serve very hot with additional pats of butter. This can be made ahead and refrigerated, covered, for a day or two and gently reheated over low heat or a water bath.

ITALIAN SAUSAGE, PEPPER, AND ONION POTATO PIE

YIELDS 8 TO 10 SERVINGS

This decadent, layered pie begins with a fat layer of mashed potatoes, a layer of mozzarella, a big layer of sautéed sausage, peppers, and onions, and is finished with more mozzarella. Hearty and comforting, it's like an Italian/American potato and cheese lasagna and requires a lot less work.

1 tablespoon butter, room temperature

1 pound (450 g) loose regular breakfast sausage

1 red bell pepper, halved, seeded, and cut into very thin strips

1 green bell pepper, halved, seeded, and cut into very thin strips

1 onion, peeled, halved, and cut into very thin strips

1 clove garlic, smashed and finely chopped

1 teaspoon fennel seeds

2 teaspoons dried oregano

1/2 teaspoon kosher or sea salt

1 teaspoon ground black pepper

1 tablespoon white wine, such as Chardonnay or Pinot Grigio,

1/2 prepared recipe Ultimate Mashed Potatoes Master Recipe—Rustic Version (page 17)

2 cups grated mozzarella, divided

Preheat oven to 375° F (190° C). Butter a 1.5-quart (1.5-l) deep casserole dish with the room-temperature butter.

Crumble the sausage into a large sauté pan heated over medium heat. Cook, stirring and breaking up with a wooden spoon, until browned, about 5 minutes. Add the bell peppers, onion, garlic, fennel seeds, oregano, salt, and pepper. Cook, stirring over medium-low heat, until the vegetables are very soft, about 20 minutes. Add the wine and cook off to a glaze. Set aside.

To compile, place mashed potatoes into the casserole dish. Level off with a spatula. Sprinkle 1 cup of the mozzarella over the top. Add the reserved sausage and pepper combination and level off with a spatula. Sprinkle the remaining mozzarella over the top. Bake for 25–30 minutes, or until the pie is bubbling and the cheese is melted and golden. Serve very hot.

GREEN PEAS AND ONION MASHED POTATOES

YIELDS 8 TO 10 SERVINGS

Sweet peas and onion chunks dance in this spring-inspired potato mash. Add a bit of fresh parsley and/or mint for additional spring pizzazz. This would be beautiful with prime rib or a grilled steak.

1 full recipe Ultimate Mashed Potatoes Master Recipe—Rustic Version (page 17)
1 small onion, peeled, halved, and thinly sliced
2 cups (300 g) peas (fresh or frozen)
1 teaspoon salt
Water

Prepare the mashed potatoes as per directions, adding the onion slices to the pot along with the potatoes and water. Cook and mash as directed until chunky smooth.

Meanwhile, place the peas in a large pot with salt and water to cover. Bring to a boil over high heat, reduce to a simmer, and cook for 10 minutes, or until the peas are softened but still retain their shape. Drain in a colander and run very cold water over them to stop the cooking and maintain the brilliant green color. Gently fold the peas into the warm potatoes and heat through over low heat. Serve hot.

POTATO AND SPINACH PHYLLO BITES

YIELDS 24 TO 26 APPETIZERS

Crispy, golden Greek phyllo pastry encases petite pillows of baked, riced potatoes with sautéed spinach and a generous dash of nutmeg in this wonderful dish. Phyllo can be difficult to work with, but if you follow the package directions (I like Athens brand) to thaw it in the refrigerator and keep it damp with a towel while you're working, it will comply. Rather than deal with folding the pastry into repeated triangles or complicated forms, here the filling is rolled with the pastry into little logs with crimped ends—resembling hard candy wrappers. The pastry ends become golden and crunchy and the inside puffy and delicious. These can be prepped ahead entirely and baked just before serving, which makes them delicious, hostess-friendly fare.

2 tablespoons unsalted butter

1/2 cup (75 g) finely chopped red onion

1 1/2 cups (230 g) thawed frozen chopped spinach

1 teaspoon kosher or sea salt

1/2 teaspoon ground black pepper

1/2 teaspoon ground nutmeg

2 cups (320 g) Basic Riced Potatoes (page 21)

1 egg, beaten

1 teaspoon kosher or sea salt

1/2 teaspoon ground black pepper

1 full roll (1/2 package) phyllo dough, thawed, unrolled, and cut vertically into 3 (4-inch / 10-cm) wide layers, covered with a damp towel

4 tablespoons unsalted butter, melted

Preheat oven to 375° F (190° C). Melt 2 tablespoons butter with the onion in a large sauté pan over medium heat until softened, about 5 minutes. Stir in the spinach, salt, pepper, and nutmeg. Reduce heat to low and cook until tender and most of the liquid has evaporated, 5–7 minutes. Set aside.

In a medium bowl, combine the potatoes, egg, salt, and pepper with a wooden spoon. Stir in the reserved spinach mixture until well incorporated. Cover and refrigerate for 15 minutes (or overnight to fill and bake the following day).

To fill the phyllo, gently pull 2 layers of the pastry from the stack. Using a pastry brush and the melted butter, generously butter the top layer. Place 1 tablespoon of the filling at the very end of the buttered layer, leaving about 1/4 inch (6 mm) free space on each side of the filling. Roll gently, as you would a cigar, until sealed. Twist the free ends as you would a hard candy wrapper. Place seam side down on a rimmed baking sheet. Continue with the rest until completed, spacing generously. Brush the tops and ends of each lightly with remaining butter and sprinkle lightly with salt. Bake for 30 minutes, or until golden brown. Arrange on a serving platter and serve hot.

CHEDDAR-BACON-CELERY SKINS

YIELDS 16 APPETIZERS

Who doesn't love an ooey-gooey, crispy, delicious potato skin to go with a great football game? These skins get a triple crisp—the initial bake, a second hollowed and buttered bake, a thin layer of leftover mashed potatoes, and then a final bake in a very hot oven. Their garnish is simply grated cheddar cheese, some bacon, and a surprise base layer of diced celery. A dollop of tangy, cool sour cream scores every time.

16 hollowed baked potato skins
   (reserved from Basic Riced
   Potatoes, page 21)
2 tablespoons unsalted butter,
   melted
Kosher or sea salt and ground black
   pepper
1 cup leftover mashed potatoes
1/2 cup (50 g) very finely chopped
   celery
8 strips bacon, fried or baked until
   crispy, drained on paper towels,
   and coarsely chopped
1 cup (120 g) grated cheddar cheese
Sour cream

Preheat oven to 500° F (260° C). Brush the skins with the butter and arrange on a baking sheet. Season each lightly with salt and pepper. Bake until crisp and golden, about 5 minutes. Remove from oven.

To fill, spoon in about 1 tablespoon of the mashed potatoes and level, sprinkle a few pieces of celery, top with a thin layer of bacon, and finally add about 1 tablespoon of cheese in each potato skin. Repeat. Sprinkle any remaining bacon on top, and bake until bubbly and hot, 8–10 minutes. Serve hot and don't forget to pass the sour cream.

POTATO, CORN, AND SALMON MUFFIN CAKES

YIELDS 24 MINI MUFFIN CAKES

Perfect party fare, these airy cakes can be prepped fully in advance and baked at the last minute. Bake in mini muffin pans or spoon into a buttered baking pan for a more casual look with just a little less work.

2 tablespoons unsalted butter, room temperature

2 cups (120 g) Basic Riced Potatoes (page 21)

1 large egg, beaten

1/2 cup (60 g) full-fat ricotta

1 teaspoon kosher or sea salt

1/2 teaspoon ground black pepper

1 cup (150 g) canned corn kernels, well-drained

1 cup (140 g) skinless, boneless canned pink salmon, well-drained (fresh salmon can be used)

1 teaspoon fresh lemon zest

1/4 cup (10 g) finely chopped fresh parsley

2 tablespoons unsalted butter, melted

Fresh lemon juice

Preheat oven to 400° F (205° C). Generously butter the cups of a 24 mini muffin pan with 2 tablespoons butter. Using a wooden spoon, combine the potatoes with the egg, ricotta, salt, and pepper until fully incorporated. Add the corn, salmon, lemon zest, and parsley, folding to combine.

Place about 2 tablespoons of the filling into each muffin cup. Press the top of each to compress and flatten slightly. Brush each with a light coating of melted butter. Bake for 40 minutes, or until golden and slightly puffed. Remove from oven and let rest for 5 minutes. Using the edge of a spoon or pastry spatula, gently remove the muffins from the pan and arrange on a serving platter. Serve hot. If desired, squeeze a little fresh lemon juice over the tops while still very hot, and just before serving.

SIMPLY SWEET POTATO SOUP

Sweet potatoes are too frequently loaded with cream, fat, and sugar that mask their subtle natural flavor and pile on calories. Not so in this silky soup where sweet potatoes simmer with complementary vegetable cousins, carrots, celery, and onion. The soup is finished with a whisper of cream, rendering it quite possibly the most delicious potato soup you will ever have the pleasure of eating. You can make it ahead and refrigerate or freeze, reheat, and add the cream just before serving.

1 tablespoon rendered bacon fat or unsalted butter

2 stalks celery, trimmed and cut into medium dice (about 1 cup / 100 g)

2 small carrots, peeled and cut into medium dice (about 1 cup / 130 g)

1 medium onion, peeled and cut into medium dice (about 1 cup / 150 g)

1 teaspoon kosher or sea salt

1/2 teaspoon ground black pepper

1 teaspoon ground ginger

1/2 teaspoon ground allspice

1 teaspoon ground cinnamon

2 large sweet potatoes, peeled and cut into 1-inch (2.5-cm) cubes (about 3 cups / 540 g)

6 cups (1.4 l) low-sodium chicken stock

2 to 3 tablespoons honey

1 tablespoon heavy cream

In a large heavy-bottom pot, melt the bacon fat over medium heat. Add the celery, carrots, onion, salt, pepper, ginger, allspice, and cinnamon. Stir to coat. Cook over medium until just softened and fragrant, about 5 minutes. Add the sweet potatoes and stock. Bring to a boil over high heat, reduce heat to low, and simmer gently, uncovered, until the potatoes are very tender and falling apart. Remove from the heat.

Purée with an immersion blender (Basic Mashing Tools, page 10) in the same pan until frothy and very smooth. Or, for an even earthier, more rustic version, mash with a manual masher (Basic Mashing Tools, page 10) until chunky smooth. Add honey to taste, bring to a simmer to heat through, and finish with the cream. Taste and adjust seasoning as needed. Serve very hot.

SAVORY SWEET POTATO BREAKFAST FLAN WITH SAGE AND SAUSAGE CRUMBLE

YIELDS 6 TO 8 SERVINGS

The morning-friendly flavors of fresh orange juice, maple syrup, and sausage make this an obvious breakfast or brunch choice, but it is savory and delicious enough to enjoy as a side or main dish of any meal. The silky flan texture from slow, gentle cooking in a water bath is just gorgeous with floating bites of sage-kissed sausage crumbles. It is as equally delicious hot from the oven as it is chilled.

1 tablespoon butter, room temperature

1 pound (450 g) mild country sausage

$1/2$ teaspoon kosher or sea salt

$1/2$ teaspoon ground black pepper

1 tablespoon rubbed dry sage leaves (or ground sage)

1 cup (255 g) cooked, mashed sweet potatoes (Basic Riced Potatoes, page 21)

$1^1/2$ cups (360 ml) half-and-half

$1/2$ cup (120 ml) real maple syrup

3 tablespoons sugar

3 large eggs

1 tablespoon fresh orange zest

1 tablespoon fresh orange juice

$1/2$ teaspoon ground cinnamon

$1/2$ teaspoon ground ginger

Pinch of ground cloves

Salt, to taste

Preheat oven to 325° F (160° C). Butter a 2-quart (2-l) baking dish with 1 tablespoon butter. Heat a large skillet over medium-high heat and crumble in the sausage, stirring with a wooden spoon to break up. Season with salt, pepper, and sage. Continue to cook until browned, about 5 minutes. Turn off heat, drain off any visible excess fat, and set aside.

Place the remaining ingredients in the bowl of a food processor fitted with a metal blade. Purée until very smooth, about 1 minute. Spread the cooked sausage in the bottom of the baking dish. Pour the custard purée over the top (some of the sausage will float). Place the dish in a large, deep roasting pan. Gently pour boiling water around the edges of the dish to halfway up the sides.

Bake for 1 hour and 30 minutes, or until a knife inserted in the center comes out clean. Remove the dish from the water, cool for 5 minutes, and serve hot with fresh sage leaves for garnish, if desired. Alternatively, bring to room temperature, cover, and refrigerate overnight before serving. Reheat gently over a water bath or serve chilled.

SWEET POTATO INDIAN PUDDING

YIELDS 6 TO 8 SERVINGS

This rustic and gorgeous dish combines elements of a traditional New England Indian pudding with ingredients widely used throughout the South—sweet potatoes and grits. If you can't find stone-ground grits, cornmeal or polenta will work fine. But skip the instant variety. Longer cooking soaks up all the flavor of the pudding and melts the corn into one integrated bowl of perfection. It's best warm with a generous scoop of vanilla ice cream or whipped cream on top.

1 tablespoon unsalted butter, room temperature

3 cups (700 ml) half-and-half

1 cup (255 g) cooked, mashed sweet potatoes (Basic Riced Potatoes, page 21)

1/3 cup (50 g) stone-ground white or yellow grits (or cornmeal)

1/4 cup (60 ml) molasses

2 large eggs

1/2 cup (110 g) firmly packed dark brown sugar

1 teaspoon kosher or sea salt

2 teaspoons real vanilla extract

1 teaspoon ground ginger

1 teaspoon ground cinnamon

2 tablespoons cold unsalted butter, cut into 1/4-inch (6-mm) cubes

Vanilla ice cream or whipped cream

Preheat oven to 350° F (175° C). Butter a 1.5- to 2-quart (1.5- to 2-l) deep-sided baking dish with 1 tablespoon butter.

Bring the half-and-half to a simmer over medium-high heat in a medium pot. Do not boil. When simmering, whisk in the sweet potatoes, grits, and molasses. Whisk constantly over medium-high heat until thickened to a thin pudding stage, about 5 minutes. Turn off heat and set aside.

In a large bowl, whisk together the eggs, brown sugar, salt, vanilla, ginger, and cinnamon until frothy. Whisk in 1 cup of the warm pudding mixture. Pour in the remaining pudding mixture and whisk to combine. Pour the pudding into the baking dish. Bake in oven on the center rack for 40 minutes.

Add the cold butter cubes, sprinkling evenly over the top. Reduce the heat to 325° F (160° C). Cook for 45–50 minutes, until a knife inserted in the center comes out clean. The pudding will quiver slightly to the touch. Remove from oven. Let rest for 10–15 minutes before serving. Serve warm with vanilla ice cream or whipped cream.

SWEET POTATO-MACADAMIA NUT ICE CREAM

The sweet potatoes give this ice cream a warm sunset hue and silky texture, while the macadamia nuts provide a crunchy finish that will not be soon forgotten.

1¼ cups (300 ml) whole milk

2 cups (475 ml) whipping cream

1 cup (255 g) cooked, mashed sweet potatoes (Basic Riced Potatoes, page 21)

¾ cup (150 g) sugar

6 egg yolks

1 teaspoon real vanilla extract

1 teaspoon pumpkin pie spice

1 teaspoon cinnamon

Pinch cloves

Pinch of kosher or sea salt

½ cup (65 g) coarsely chopped salted macadamia nuts

Bring the milk and cream to an aggressive simmer in a saucepan over medium-high heat. In a large bowl, whisk together the sweet potatoes, sugar, and egg yolks until frothy. Whisk in the vanilla, pumpkin pie spice, cinnamon, cloves, and salt until smooth. Once the milk and cream have come to a simmer, slowly whisk into the egg mixture, stirring constantly. Return the entire mixture to the saucepan and cook over medium heat, stirring constantly with a wooden spoon. The custard is done once it starts to coat the back of the spoon and bubbles on top have disappeared, about 5 minutes.

Remove from the heat and strain through a fine-mesh strainer into a bowl set onto a bed of ice; let cool completely, stirring occasionally. Freeze in an ice cream maker according to manufacturer's directions. Add the macadamia nuts once the ice cream is halfway set and still fairly soft, about 12 minutes into the freezing process.

Serve plain, or garnish with additional chopped macadamia nuts and whipped cream for garnish.

VEGETABLE MASHES

Any time of year is a great time of year to indulge in the comforting, fulfilling essence of delicious mashed goodness, yet each season affords a marvelous and different variety of colors and textures to choose from. Summer's delicate tomatoes, corn, squashes, and cucumbers, while wonderful in their raw and simplest states, are also magnificent roasted, as in the Roasted Tomato Pizza Panzanella (page 74), and blended with cheese, cream, and fresh thyme, as in the smashing Cheddar Two-Summer-Squash Mash (page 69). Cucumbers chill out Greek style in the zesty Chilled and Dilled Tzatziki Soup (page 86).

As we turn the pages into fall, vegetables deepen in color and flavor, seemingly seasoned by the vibrant hues of autumn leaves. Creamy-white, nutty, and slightly peppery parsnips glow in their simplicity in Purely Parsnip Purée with Browned-Butter Pecan Sauce (page 98, and cauliflower embraces decadence in the irresistible Roasted Cauliflower and Cheddar Soup with Bacon Crumble (page 89). Winter's inevitable chill is squashed with the likes of soothing Maple Acorn Squash Soup (page 97) and belly-warming Butternut–Baby Kale Shells and Cheese Bake (page 106).

Finally, the freshness of spring is celebrated in Minty Spring Pea Lettuce Wraps (page 113) and a radiant Roasted Beet and Sour Cream Dill Mash (page 117). Carrots get spicy with gingery heat in Ginger and Cumin–Spiced Carrot Mash (page 114), and fresh spring onions are creamed to delicate perfection in Creamed Onion Soup (page 118).

SUMMER

CHEDDAR TWO-SUMMER-SQUASH MASH

YIELDS 6 SERVINGS

Summer squash, slightly sweet and squeaks-in-your-teeth fresh at peak summer season, is one of my favorite summer treats. Often, I'll sauté either yellow summer squash or zucchini in a little olive oil with some red onion, finish it with a sprinkle of fresh basil and grated Parmesan, and call it a summer's night. However, the two squashes marry beautifully together, as they do in this mash casserole, which resonates with the lemony freshness of thyme. The texture is airy and light, almost mousse-like, topped with a buttery panko bread crumb crunch. While you can substitute unseasoned traditional bread crumbs, panko delivers a crunchy edge (and it's really worth having in your pantry at all times). The casserole is delicious hot, warm, or even room temperature.

2 medium zucchini, ends trimmed and cut into 1-inch (2.5-cm) dice (about 3 cups / 370 g)

3 medium yellow summer squash, ends trimmed and cut into 1-inch (2.5-cm) dice (about 4 cups / 495 g)

Water

3 1/2 teaspoons kosher or sea salt, divided

1 1/2 tablespoons finely chopped fresh thyme leaves

1 cup (240 ml) full-fat sour cream

2 cups (240 g) grated mild cheddar cheese

1 small shallot, finely chopped (about 2 tablespoons)

1 teaspoon ground black pepper

1 egg, beaten

Pinch of ground nutmeg

3 tablespoons unsalted butter, divided

1 cup panko bread crumbs or unseasoned traditional bread crumbs

Pinch of ground black pepper and kosher or sea salt

Preheat oven to 350° F (175° C). Place the zucchini and summer squash in a medium saucepan. Pour in enough water to barely cover and add 2 teaspoons salt. Bring to a boil, reduce to a simmer, and cook, uncovered, until the squash is very tender, about 20 minutes. Drain very well in a colander, gently pressing out any excess water, and return to the pan.

Mash with a manual masher (Basic Mashing Tools, page 10) until the squash is chunky smooth. With a wooden spoon, blend in the thyme, sour cream, cheese, shallot, pepper, remaining salt, egg, and nutmeg. Pour into a medium casserole dish that has been greased with 1 tablespoon butter, spreading with spoon to even the top.

Melt the remaining butter in a medium saucepan over medium-high heat. Add the panko and seasoning and toss to coat. Brown the crumbs to a golden brown, being careful to toss and avoid burning. Spread the bread crumbs evenly over the top.

Bake for 45 minutes, uncovered, or until bubbly and golden brown. Let rest for 10 minutes before serving and garnish with some fresh thyme sprigs. This makes a lovely meal with a green salad and fresh bread and butter. The casserole can be assembled ahead, refrigerated, and baked just before serving.

AVOCADO MASH WITH RED PEPPER FLAKES, RED ONION, AND RADISH TOASTS

YIELDS 8 SERVINGS

Avocados are available year-round, but are mostly thought of as warm-weather fare. This delicious and nutritious riff on guacamole gets a speck of heat from red pepper flakes and pumped-up color and crunch from fresh red onion and radishes. Serve it on thick slabs of toasted multi-grain bread for a maximum-nutrition breakfast (or snack) punch that will keep you energized for hours. Keep in mind that avocados discolor when exposed to air. It's important to get the lemon juice into the mash immediately, which helps prevent discoloration. Also, make within a few hours of service time and store with plastic wrap pressed against the top of the mash so it cannot be exposed to air. It's best to serve immediately, however, and at room temperature.

2 ripe Hass avocados, halved and pits removed (page 13)

Juice of 1/2 lemon (about 2 tablespoons)

1 tablespoon fruity extra virgin olive oil

Pinch of crushed red pepper flakes

1/2 teaspoon kosher or sea salt

1/4 teaspoon ground black pepper

1/3 cup (50 g) finely chopped red onion

3 radishes, finely chopped (about 1/3 cup / 40 g)

2 cloves garlic, smashed and very finely chopped

8 slices multi-grain bread, cut on the diagonal and toasted

Delicately scoop the flesh of the avocado out of each half and place in a bowl. Mash, using a fork or manual masher (Basic Mashing Tools, page 10), with the lemon juice, olive oil, red pepper flakes, salt, and pepper. Stir in the onion, radishes, and garlic to combine. Cover tightly (against the mash) with plastic wrap and keep at room temperature for up to 3 hours, or refrigerate overnight.

BUTTER BEAN AND SMOKED HAM HOCK MASH

YIELDS 4 TO 6 SERVINGS

Butter beans are plump lime-green nuggets of southern goodness that start bursting out of the ground once the heat turns up in mid and late summer. They are aptly named; their taste is smooth and mild, not too far removed from butter. Baby lima beans are very similar and easily found in other regions or in your grocer's freezer. Smoked ham hocks simmer together with the fresh beans to develop a fragrant broth that is later re-mashed into the mix, while any remnants of edible meat are removed from the hock and returned to the mix. Simply delicious!

1 large smoked ham hock (about
  $1/2$ pound / 230 g)
5 cups (1 kg) fresh or frozen butter
  beans or baby lima beans
1 shallot, peeled and quartered
Water
1 teaspoon kosher or sea salt
1 teaspoon ground black pepper
1 tablespoon fresh lemon juice
3 tablespoons unsalted butter, room
  temperature
Handful fresh parsley leaves
Kosher or sea salt and ground black
  pepper, to taste

Place the ham hock, beans, and shallot in a large saucepan and add just enough water to cover; add salt and pepper. Bring to a boil over high heat, reduce to medium low, and simmer, uncovered, for 20 minutes until the beans are very tender. Drain in a colander over a large bowl, reserving 2 cups (475 ml) of the cooking liquid. Remove and reserve the ham hock.

Place the beans and shallot in the bowl of a food processor fitted with a metal blade; add lemon juice, butter, and parsley. While pulsing, stream the reserved liquid through the mouth of the processor. The mash should be fluffy, light, and a refreshing green color. For a more rustic version, mash with a manual masher (Basic Mashing Tools, page 10) in a large bowl, folding in about 2 tablespoons finely chopped fresh parsley at the end. Taste and adjust salt and pepper as needed.

Cut off skin and fat from the hock and reserve any slivers of pink flesh. There should be about $1/4$ to $1/2$ cup (35 to 70 g). Use as a garnish on the top of each serving, or mix into the mash. Serve immediately while hot, or store refrigerated, covered, overnight and reheat over a water bath or low heat.

ROASTED TOMATO PIZZA PANZANELLA

Toasted cubes of artisan bread are bathed in a potent and sweet acidic mash of roasted tomatoes, balsamic vinegar, fresh herbs, and more, then tossed with the familiar flavors of pizza: pepperoni, fresh mozzarella, garlic, and bell peppers. The result is a bowlful of this Italian bread salad (panzanella) classic, but with a fabulous pizza twist. This will take center stage at any party or buffet and make a festive and complete dinner with a small green salad. It's better to let the flavors develop for up to 20 minutes, but do not wait longer than an hour to serve, as it risks turning the appealing crunch of the bread to mush.

TOMATOES

8 Roma tomatoes, halved vertically

1 teaspoon extra virgin olive oil

Generous pinch of kosher or sea salt and ground black pepper

BREAD

1 large day-old white French baguette or boule, cut into 1-inch (2.5-cm) cubes (about 7 cups / 245 g)

3 tablespoons extra virgin olive oil

1 teaspoon kosher or sea salt

1 teaspoon ground pepper

1 teaspoon dried oregano

TO ASSEMBLE

2 large cloves garlic, smashed and finely chopped

2 tablespoons extra virgin olive oil

1 tablespoon aged balsamic vinegar

1/2 cup (120 ml) low-sodium chicken or vegetable stock

1 cup (130 g) 1/2-inch (13-mm) pepperoni cubes

Reserved bread

1/4 cup (10 g) coarsely chopped fresh parsley

1 tablespoon finely chopped fresh rosemary

1 red or yellow bell pepper, cored, seeded, and cut into 1/2-inch (13-mm) dice

1/2 cup (75 g) finely chopped red onion

1 cup (110 g) drained fresh mozzarella, cut into 1/2-inch (13-mm) dice

Kosher or sea salt and ground black pepper, to taste

Preheat oven to 425° F (220° C). On a baking sheet, toss the tomatoes with olive oil, salt, and pepper, coating evenly. Arrange the tomatoes, cut side down. Roast until the tomatoes have softened and shrunk in size by about half, stirring once or twice to prevent sticking, about 40 minutes. Remove from the oven and set aside.

Separately, arrange the bread cubes on another baking sheet and toss to coat with olive oil, salt, pepper, and oregano. Roast until golden brown and crispy, stirring once, about 20 minutes. Remove from oven and set aside.

In a large bowl, mash the warm tomatoes and all of their juices with a manual masher (Basic Mashing Tools, page 10). Whisk in garlic, olive oil, vinegar, and stock. Add the remaining ingredients and toss thoroughly to coat. Taste and adjust salt and pepper. Reserve at room temperature for at least 20 minutes before serving. The panzanella can be covered and refrigerated for up to 1 hour. Bring to room temperature before serving.

SAVORY SUMMER CORN AND SHRIMP PUDDING

This fluffy, soufflé-like pudding brings summer corn glory to a new level. It involves a few steps, but the béchamel, a white sauce lightly bound with eggs and dotted with roasted poblano chile pepper and bites of sweet shrimp, is well worth the work. Delicious hot, room temperature, or cold for a surprise breakfast treat, it will become a regular on your summer table. Use the freshest corn and shrimp you can find. It will make a difference. Use a large shallow baking pan, which will allow the pudding to cook in less time and prevents the shrimp from becoming tough.

6 cups (900 g) fresh or frozen corn kernels

2 teaspoons kosher or sea salt

1 teaspoon ground black pepper

Water

1 large poblano chile pepper

BÉCHAMEL AND FINISHING

5 tablespoons unsalted butter, divided

3 tablespoons all-purpose flour

2 1/2 cups (595 ml) reserved corn cooking liquid

1/4 cup (60 ml) half-and-half

Light pinch of kosher or sea salt and ground black pepper

2 eggs, beaten

1/4 cup (30 g) full-fat ricotta

1/2 pound (230 g), 21 to 25 count peeled and deveined raw shrimp, cut into 1/2-inch (13-mm) dice

4 scallions, green part only, finely chopped

1/4 cup (10 g) finely chopped fresh basil

Kosher or sea salt and ground black pepper, to taste

Preheat oven to 350° F (175° C). Place the corn in a large saucepan with salt and pepper and just enough water to barely cover. Bring to a boil over high heat and reduce to a simmer over medium low. Cook uncovered, until the corn is tender, about 12 minutes. Drain the corn in a colander over a large bowl. Set aside, reserving the liquid.

Meanwhile, place the poblano under a hot broiler or over an open flame on your stove. Roast, turning occasionally, to char the skin all over so that it is black and blistered. Run under cool water, peel off the charred skin, and open to remove seeds. Cut into small dice and reserve.

In the same pan used to cook the corn, melt 3 tablespoons butter over medium heat to make the béchamel. Add flour, stirring to combine, and cook for another 1–2 minutes over medium-low heat. Whisk in reserved corn cooking liquid, and bring to a boil over medium-high heat, whisking constantly. Reduce to a simmer over medium low and cook until thickened, about 5 minutes. Whisk in the half-and-half, salt, pepper, and remaining butter. Whisk to combine and set aside.

Place the reserved corn in the bowl of a food processor fitted with a metal blade. Stream in the béchamel while the processor is running. Pulse just 10–15 times until the sauce is incorporated and the corn is chunky smooth. Pour the mixture into a large bowl. Alternatively, place the same ingredients into a large bowl and mash vigorously with a manual masher (Basic Mashing Tools, page 10), scraping down the sides and bottom.

Whisk in the eggs and ricotta to incorporate. Stir in the shrimp, reserved poblano, scallions, and basil. Taste and adjust seasoning as needed. Grease a large shallow casserole pan with butter. Pour in the pudding and bake until set, 50 minutes to 1 hour. Serve warm, room temperature, or cold. Garnish with fresh basil leaves, if desired.

ROASTED EGGPLANT BABA GHANOUSH

YIELDS 2 1/2 CUPS (600 G)

This Levantine dip and condiment (pronounced baba gahnoosh) means "pampered papa" in Arabic. It's common on Middle Eastern restaurant menus, but it's surprisingly difficult to find a truly excellent version. This one is. The key is to drain off the bitter juices that seep from the roasted eggplant as it cools and to get the right ratio of tahini (sesame seed butter, usually found near the peanut butter at the grocery store) to eggplant. Also, use your very best quality olive oil to finish. The fruity flavors will really shine through and complement the eggplant. You'll love this fluffy, flavorful vegan dip served with the Homemade Pita Chip recipe that follows.

1 large eggplant, halved vertically

1 clove garlic, smashed and chopped

1 teaspoon kosher or sea salt

1/2 teaspoon ground black pepper

2 tablespoons fresh lemon juice

2 tablespoons tahini

2 tablespoons coarsely chopped parsley

1 tablespoon fruity extra virgin olive oil

Preheat oven to 425° F (220° C). Place the eggplant, cut side down, on a baking sheet. Roast for 45 minutes to 1 hour, or until the eggplant has softened and dimpled. Remove from oven and cool for 15–20 minutes. Drain and discard any liquid that has pooled on the baking sheet.

Gently scoop the eggplant flesh away from the skin and into the bowl of a food processor fitted with a metal blade, being careful to remove all of the flesh and avoid including the bitter skin. Add the garlic, salt, and pepper and process until smooth. Add the lemon juice, tahini, parsley, and olive oil. Process again, until light and fluffy. Taste and adjust seasonings as needed.

You can prepare this recipe using a manual masher (Basic Mashing Tools, page 10) by mashing and really smashing the eggplant with the other ingredients, streaming in the olive oil as you go. Pull the eggplant apart by stretching the sometimes-stringy pulp with the base of your masher. The texture will be a little more rustic than the food processor version, but still very delicious. Serve in a bowl at room temperature with Homemade Pita Chips.

continued>

HOMEMADE PITA CHIPS

YIELDS 32 CHIPS

Select a thinner variety of commercial pita bread to make these crispy, delicious chips. They're best still warm from the oven and served with many of the dips in this book.

4 pitas
3 tablespoons olive oil
1 teaspoon kosher or sea salt
1 teaspoon ground black pepper
1 tablespoon fresh parsley leaves

Preheat oven to 425° F (220° C). Cut each pita in half. Then cut each half into 4 triangles, for a total of 8 wedges per pocket. Place on a baking sheet, toss thoroughly to coat with the remaining ingredients, and arrange in a single layer. Roast for 8–10 minutes, just until they've started to brown. Turn the chips over with a spatula and bake for another 5 minutes, until very golden brown and crisp. Drain on paper towels and serve while still warm. The chips can be made ahead, fully cooled, and stored in a sealed container for up to 2 days. Re-crisp in a 425° F (220° C) oven, if desired.

SAVORY ROASTED EGGPLANT AND GARLIC BAKLAVA

YIELDS 12 TO 16 APPETIZERS

This savory take on the sweet, flaky, nutty, buttery Greek dessert classic is compiled of thin layers of roasted eggplant and garlic that have been puréed and seasoned with just a bit of lemon and honey, and very little else, and topped with a macadamia nut crumble. It makes a beautiful appetizer any time of the year, but is especially appealing on a cool summer night and delicious with sparkling wine or Champagne.

Remember to take the phyllo out of the freezer to thaw overnight in the refrigerator. Keeping the pastry covered with a damp cloth as you work makes assembly a snap. Also, keep the layers of purée very fine and even to ensure crispiness in every bite.

2 large eggplants, halved vertically

1 head garlic

2 tablespoons olive oil, divided

1 teaspoon fresh lemon juice

1 teaspoon honey

1/2 teaspoon kosher or sea salt

1/2 teaspoon ground black pepper

1 full roll (1/2 package) phyllo dough

1/4 cup (60 ml) fruity extra virgin olive oil

1/2 cup (65 g) very finely chopped macadamia nuts

Pinch of kosher or sea salt and freshly ground black pepper

Preheat oven to 425° F (220° C). Place the eggplants, cut side down, on a baking sheet greased with 1 tablespoon olive oil. Cut 1/4 inch (6 mm) off the top of the garlic to reveal the cloves, and drizzle with the remaining 1 tablespoon olive oil. Wrap the entire head with aluminum foil and place on the sheet with the eggplant. Roast until the eggplants are starting to collapse and both the garlic and eggplants are tender, about 1 hour. Remove from the oven and set aside.

When cool enough to handle, scoop the soft flesh of the eggplants into the bowl of a food processor fitted with a metal blade. Gently squeeze the flesh from the garlic casing by squeezing with hands and fingertips into the bowl of the food processor, discarding the skins. Purée the eggplants and garlic with the lemon juice, honey, salt, and pepper until smooth.

continued>

Reduce oven to 350° F (175° C) (you can make the purée ahead and refrigerate until ready to assemble). Use 2 sheets of phyllo to make a layer and place on a baking sheet. Brush a very thin coat of the olive oil over the phyllo with a pastry brush. Spread very gently and evenly with 2 tablespoons of the purée, and make the spread very thin and even. Top with another 2 sheets of phyllo and then the purée, repeating until the pastry and purée are gone. You should have 8–10 layers. Brush a final layer of the olive oil on top and sprinkle with the macadamia nuts. Season lightly with salt and pepper. Bake for 40–45 minutes, until golden brown and crunchy.

Cut into 4-inch (10-cm) squares and serve hot. Add a sprinkle of fresh chopped parsley, if desired.

ROASTED RED PEPPER AND FETA WHIP

YIELDS 2 CUPS (500 G)

Bright and bouncy, this colorful dip hits sweet and acidic notes with balsamic vinegar, lemon, fresh basil, and smoky roasted peppers. Salty, tangy feta runs through it, making it the perfect summer dip that comes together in minutes. You can save even more time by buying smoked or charred red peppers in a jar, but I prefer making them at home for maximum flavor. Char them on the grill, under the broiler, or over the open flame on a gas stove. Serve it as a dip with pita chips, but it also makes a beautiful spread on a roast beef or turkey sandwich for fresh flavor and color.

4 red bell peppers
Juice of 1/2 lemon (about
   2 tablespoons)
1 tablespoon fruity extra virgin
   olive oil
2 tablespoons balsamic vinegar
1 clove garlic, smashed and chopped
1/2 teaspoon kosher or sea salt
1/4 teaspoon ground black pepper
1 cup (245 g) 1-inch (2.5-cm) cubes
   feta cheese
1/2 teaspoon ground cumin
8 fresh basil leaves

Char the whole peppers on an open grill or under a broiler set on high heat. Turn to char each side, turning only when fully charred and blistered. Remove from the heat source. When cool enough to handle, peel the charred skin off each pepper, running under cool water to help loosen and rinse away the skin. At the same time, open the pepper and remove the seeds and any white flesh.

Place the peppers in the bowl of a food processor fitted with a metal blade. Add the lemon juice, olive oil, vinegar, garlic, salt, and pepper. Process until very smooth. Add the feta, cumin, and basil. Pulse 10 times to just incorporate. For a manual mash version, first coarsely chop the roasted peppers. Place them and everything but the basil into a large bowl and mash very vigorously to break up the peppers and incorporate the remaining ingredients. Cut the basil into a chiffonade (page 12), or very finely chop, and fold in to finish. The dip is best served at room temperature, but it can be refrigerated, covered, for up to 2 days before serving.

CHILLED AND DILLED TZATZIKI SOUP

YIELDS 6 TO 8 SERVINGS

This classic gyro topper gets a thinning new spin in this creamy, tangy soup, thickened with cooling puréed and frothy fresh cucumbers and dill. It takes just minutes to make and is super cool to eat on the hottest dog days of the summer months. The colors and flavors complement salmon especially well. Serve a grilled fillet alongside for the perfect summer feast. Keep the soup in the refrigerator for 1–2 hours before serving to fully develop the flavors and the chill.

3 large cucumbers, peeled, seeded, and cut into 1-inch (2.5-cm) lengths (about 5 cups / 660 g)

2 cloves garlic, smashed

1/2 small red onion, peeled and quartered (about 1 cup / 150 g)

2 cups (570 g) plain whole-milk Greek yogurt

1 cup (230 g) full-fat sour cream

Juice of 1/2 lemon (about 2 tablespoons)

1 1/2 teaspoons kosher or sea salt

1 teaspoon ground black pepper

1 cup fresh dill fronds (discard tough stems), coarsely chopped

Place all of the ingredients except the fresh dill in the bowl of a food processor fitted with a metal blade. Process until puréed and frothy, scraping down once or twice with a spatula to ensure all of the larger pieces have been smoothly incorporated. Add the fresh dill and pulse 10 times to incorporate. Chill completely before serving. Taste and adjust seasonings before serving; chilling will have a quieting effect on the salt and pepper.

AUTUMN & WINTER

ROASTED CAULIFLOWER AND CHEDDAR SOUP WITH BACON CRUMBLE

YIELDS 6 TO 8 SERVINGS

Roasting takes the nutty, buttery earthiness of cauliflower and transforms it into heaven, especially with a bit of cream and, of course, the background notes and assertive topping of bacon. This soup is a magical way to say hello to the cooling weather and cuddle around a warming bowl as the days grow shorter.

1 large head cauliflower, base leaves and core removed, broken into florets

1 to 2 tablespoons olive oil

Kosher or sea salt and ground black pepper, to taste

8 strips bacon, cut into ¼-inch (6-mm) dice

1 shallot, finely chopped

1 leek, white part only, cut into medium dice

1 stalk celery, cut into medium dice

¼ cup (60 ml) white wine, such as Chardonnay or Pinot Grigio

3 tablespoons all-purpose flour

4 cups (950 ml) low-sodium chicken or vegetable stock

1 teaspoon kosher or sea salt

½ teaspoon ground black pepper

1 cup (240 ml) half-and-half

¾ cup (30 g) finely chopped fresh parsley

1 cup (120 g) grated cheddar cheese

Preheat oven to 425° F (220° C). Break the cauliflower florets into smaller pieces and arrange on a baking sheet. Toss with the olive oil and dust with salt and pepper. Roast, tossing occasionally, for 25 minutes, or until the cauliflower starts turning golden and slightly softened. Remove from oven and set aside.

Meanwhile, heat a large soup pot over medium-high heat. Add the bacon. Stir to distribute evenly across the pot and break up the dice. Cook until crisp, browned, and most of the fat has rendered, about 10 minutes. Remove with a slotted spoon and drain the bacon on paper towels.

Reduce the heat to medium low. Add the shallot, leek, celery, and salt and pepper, to taste. Stir to coat. Cook until softened, about 5 minutes. Add the wine and increase heat to medium high. Cook until the wine is almost fully reduced. Add the flour, stir, and cook for 1 minute. Add the cauliflower, stock, salt, and pepper. Bring to a boil over high heat and reduce heat to medium low. Simmer for 20 minutes, or until cauliflower is softened. Remove the pot from the stove. Using an immersion blender (Basic Mashing Tools, page 10), blend the soup until smooth and frothy. Add the half-and-half, parsley, and cheese and heat through over medium heat. Adjust seasoning to taste. Serve hot with a generous crumble of the bacon.

BUTTERY PARSLEY RUTABAGA MASH

Knobby, humble rutabaga is transformed into nutty, buttery elegance in this sunset-yellow mash, which is lightened by a bit of Yukon Gold potato and made silky with butter, cream, and flecks of fresh parsley. Super easy to prepare ahead and reheat, it is a star at all holiday and entertainment tables, including mine.

1 medium rutabaga

2 small Yukon Gold potatoes, peeled and cut into 2-inch (5-cm) cubes (about 1 1/2 cups / 270 g)

1 tablespoon kosher or sea salt

Water

TO FINISH

1 cup (230 g) sour cream

3 tablespoons unsalted butter

Salt and ground black pepper, to taste

3 tablespoons finely chopped fresh parsley

Using a sharp paring knife, remove the outer thin skin as well as the tough 1/4-inch (6-mm) thick inner skin of the rutabaga. Cut into 2-inch (5-cm) cubes and place in a medium pot with the potatoes. Add enough water to cover and 1 tablespoon salt. Bring to a boil, reduce to simmer, and cook until the potatoes and rutabaga are soft, about 35 minutes.

Strain in a colander and return to the pan with the sour cream, butter, salt, and pepper. Mash using a manual masher (Basic Mashing Tools, page 10) until chunky smooth. Heat through over medium heat, stir in parsley, and adjust seasoning as needed. Serve warm. This dish is excellent with pork or chicken or on its own with a melting pat of butter on top.

NUTTY SOUTHERN-STYLE HUBBARD SQUASH MASH AND CANDIED PECAN CRUNCH

YIELDS 4 SERVINGS

This beautiful sage-green winter squash has experienced a bit of a renaissance in recent years and is increasingly available at markets throughout the cooler season. Its flesh is a deep burnt-orange color when cooked and has a nutty, rich flavor. A sweet, hot pecan crunch on top delivers the perfect texture contrast finish.

1 medium Hubbard squash or
butternut or turban squash

CANDIED PECAN CRUNCH

1 tablespoon unsalted butter
3 tablespoons dark brown sugar
1/2 cup (60 g) coarsely chopped
pecans
1/2 teaspoon ground ginger
Generous pinch of ground chipotle
Generous pinch of kosher or sea salt

TO FINISH

1/2 cup (115 g) sour cream
1 teaspoon kosher or sea salt
1/2 teaspoon ground black pepper
2 tablespoons unsalted butter
1 tablespoon real maple syrup

Preheat oven to 425° F (220° C). Cut the squash in half horizontally. Scoop out the seeds and discard. Place the squash, cut side down, on a baking sheet and bake until tender, about 45 minutes. Remove from oven and set aside.

Meanwhile, prepare the nut crunch. Melt the butter and brown sugar together, stirring, over medium-high heat in a medium saucepan. When bubbling, stir in the pecans, ginger, chipotle, and salt. Stir to coat and cook for another 2 minutes, until golden brown and caramelized. Turn out onto your cutting board and cool.

To finish the mash, scoop the cooled cooked flesh of the squash into a medium saucepan. Add the sour cream, salt, pepper, butter, and maple syrup. Stir and heat through over medium heat. Taste and adjust seasoning. Lightly chop the cooled nuts. Serve the mash immediately with a generous dusting of the candied pecans on top. The mash can be made ahead and refrigerated for up to 3 days. Reheat gently before serving. Store the nuts separately in an airtight container.

CREAMY FENNEL AND LEEK MASH WITH ORANGE AND PASTIS

YIELDS 6 TO 8 SERVINGS

Pastis is the darling of Provence in the South of France as a snappy licorice-laced aperitif, but it doubles as the ideal flavor enhancer of fennel, which has a more subtle licorice aroma. Orange and the mild onion flavor and creamy color of leeks make this a particularly festive mash, well-suited to any holiday table, and beautifully paired with roasted chicken, turkey, or pork. This mash is thickened with Arborio rice, which is the same rice used to make risotto. Feel free to substitute basmati. Be careful to stir along the way, especially at the end, which is when the rice drinks up most of the cooking liquid, making the mash susceptible to burning.

2 large fennel bulbs, stalks removed (reserve fronds for garnish), quartered, cored, and cut into 2-inch (5-cm) chunks (about 6 cups / 520 g)

2 leeks, trimmed to 1 inch (2.5 cm) above the white base, cleaned, halved vertically, and cut into 2-inch (5-cm) chunks (about 2 cups / 180 g)

2 cups (475 ml) half-and-half

1 cup (240 ml) low-sodium vegetable stock or water

2/3 cup (120 g) Arborio rice

Zest of 1 orange

1 1/2 teaspoons kosher or sea salt

1 teaspoon ground black pepper

1 tablespoon pastis

2 tablespoons unsalted butter, room temperature (optional)

Place all of the ingredients except the butter into a large saucepan. Stir to combine. Bring to a boil over high heat, reduce to a simmer, and cook, uncovered, for 30 minutes, or until the fennel, leeks, and rice are very tender and the rice has absorbed about half the liquid. Stir every 5–10 minutes to prevent rice from sticking and to adjust the vegetables in the pot so they are evenly covered. Remove from heat.

Spoon into the bowl of a food processor fitted with a metal blade. Process until chunky smooth. Taste and adjust seasoning as needed. Finish by pulsing in the butter. Serve warm and garnish with a flutter of finely chopped reserved fennel fronds. Alternatively, the whole mixture can be aggressively mashed with a manual masher (Basic Mashing Tools, page 10) in the same cooking pot. Whisk in the butter to finish. This dish can be made a day or two ahead and stored, covered, in the refrigerator. Reheat over medium-low heat.

MAPLE ACORN SQUASH SOUP

One of my favorite treats as a child was my mother's maple syrup and butter-filled baked acorn squash halves. This delicious soup is a play on the theme, except maple syrup and butter get cooked into the actual soup. Soulful and heart-warming, this soup is a wonderful way to embrace a chilly evening. Do use real maple syrup. It makes a huge difference in the authenticity of the soup's flavor.

2 large acorn squash, halved horizontally and seeded

2 tablespoons unsalted butter

1 large shallot, finely chopped

2 stalks celery, finely chopped

1-inch (2.5-cm) fresh ginger, peeled and halved vertically

Generous pinch of kosher or sea salt and ground black pepper

2 teaspoons ground cinnamon

2 tablespoons bourbon

4 cups (950 ml) low-sodium vegetable stock

1 cup (240 ml) water

1/4 cup (60 ml) plus 2 tablespoons real maple syrup

2 teaspoons kosher or sea salt

1 teaspoon ground black pepper

2 tablespoons heavy cream

3 tablespoons finely chopped chives

Preheat oven to 425° F (220° C). Place the acorn squash, cut side down, on a baking sheet. Roast for 50 minutes to 1 hour, or until the flesh is very tender. Set aside to cool. When cool enough to handle, scoop the flesh from the interior of the squash, discarding the shells. You should have about 4 cups (980 g).

In a large soup pot, melt the butter over medium heat. Add the shallot and celery and cook for 5 minutes, stirring, until just softened. Add the ginger, salt, pepper, cinnamon, and bourbon; stir to combine. Cook until the bourbon has reduced to a glaze, about 3 minutes. Add the stock, water, squash, maple syrup, salt, and pepper. Bring to a boil over high and reduce to a simmer, cooking, uncovered, for 20 minutes. Remove ginger pieces and discard.

In the same pot, purée the soup with an immersion blender (Basic Mashing Tools, page 10) until very smooth. Finish with the cream, heating through. Taste and adjust seasonings as needed. Serve hot in individual soup bowls garnished with a flutter of fresh chives.

PURELY PARSNIP PURÉE WITH BROWNED-BUTTER PECAN SAUCE

YIELDS 8 TO 10 SERVINGS

Parsnips, long undervalued for their humble root vegetable origins, have recently come back into cooking vogue, and with just cause. A member of the carrot family, the creamy white and pale-yellow hues of the parsnips, and the distinctive peppery, sweet, and nutty flavor lend themselves to many delicious preparations. This stunning side, as the name implies, is all about the parsnips. The browned butter sauce and pecan topping is the perfect counter to the pure parsnip sweetness and airy texture of the purée.

3 large parsnips, peeled and cut into
   2-inch (5-cm) chunks

3 tablespoons olive oil

1 teaspoon kosher or sea salt

1 teaspoon ground black pepper

1 cup (240 ml) low-sodium
   vegetable stock

½ cup (120 ml) half-and-half

⅓ cup (75 g) full-fat sour cream

BROWNED-BUTTER PECAN SAUCE

4 tablespoons unsalted butter

1 cup (120 g) coarsely chopped
   pecans

Pinch of kosher or sea salt and
   ground black pepper

Preheat oven to 425° F (220° C). Place the parsnips on a baking sheet and toss to coat with the olive oil, salt, and pepper. Arrange in a single layer and bake 45 minutes, stirring once or twice, until very soft and slightly golden. While still very hot, place in the bowl of a food processor fitted with a metal blade. Purée until creamy smooth with the stock, half-and-half, and sour cream. Taste and adjust seasoning as needed. If you like, a manual masher (Basic Mashing Tools, page 10) will do the job just as well. Mash away in the same cooking pot, pressing down and stirring to aerate as much as possible. Keep warm over gentle heat or a simmering water bath.

Meanwhile, melt the butter in a medium sauté pan over medium-high heat. Add the pecans and toss to coat. Continue cooking until the butter has begun to brown and bubble and the nuts are toasted, about 5 minutes, tossing the nuts every 30 seconds. Season lightly with salt and pepper. Serve the nuts and butter sauce drizzled over bowls of the warm parsnips. The purée and nut sauce can be made a day or two ahead and stored separately in the refrigerator. Reheat separately to serve.

ROASTED PUMPKIN PIE BREAD PUDDING

YIELDS 10 TO 12 SERVINGS

A little bit pumpkin pie, a little bit bread pudding, this delightful custard is plumped up with small cubes of day-old bread and sweet, nutty roasted pumpkin. Be sure to use the pie pumpkins usually available around Halloween and Thanksgiving and day-old bread to soak up all of the silky custard. Served individually in ramekins or custard cups, it's delicious hot, warm, or even cold with a big scoop of vanilla ice cream.

1 medium pie pumpkin, halved horizontally and seeded

6 large eggs

2½ cups (595 ml) half-and-half

1 cup (220 g) firmly packed light brown sugar

1 tablespoon real vanilla extract

1 teaspoon kosher or sea salt

1 tablespoon ground cinnamon

1 teaspoon ground ginger

½ teaspoon ground nutmeg

¼ teaspoon allspice

1 whole day-old white French baguette, cut into ½-inch (13-mm) cubes (about 6 cups / 210 g)

2 tablespoons unsalted butter, room temperature

Preheat oven to 425° F (220° C). Place the pumpkin, cut side down, on a baking sheet. Roast for 60–75 minutes, until soft and imploded. Remove from oven and set aside to cool. When cool enough to handle, scoop the flesh from the skins into a medium bowl and discard the skins. This can be done a day or two ahead and stored, covered, in the refrigerator.

Reduce oven to 350° F (175° C). In a large bowl, mash 2½ cups (610 g) of the pumpkin flesh with a manual masher (Basic Mashing Tools, page 10) until smooth. Add the eggs and half-and-half and whisk until thoroughly combined. Whisk in the brown sugar, vanilla, salt, cinnamon, ginger, nutmeg, and allspice. Add the bread cubes and stir to combine. Let set at room temperature, stirring once or twice, for 20 minutes, or until the bread has absorbed most of the custard.

Butter 10 to 12 (1-cup) custard cups or ramekins liberally with the butter. Ladle equal parts custard and bread into each cup. Arrange on a baking sheet and bake until set and golden, about 40 minutes. Remove from oven and serve hot, warm, or cold (they will store a few days, covered, in the refrigerator) with a big scoop of vanilla ice cream.

CHRISTMAS GUACAMOLE WITH POMEGRANATE AND ORANGE

YIELDS ABOUT 2 CUPS (450 G)

The shimmering ruby-red and jewel-like arils of winter's pomegranate shine against the backdrop of the mellow green of creamy avocado in this so-good-you-cannot-stop-eating-it holiday treat. Packed with three super foods and magnificent fruity flavors, it's also nothing to feel guilty about when going back for more. Make up to 1 hour before serving (to prevent discoloration) and serve room temperature with warm Homemade Pita Chips (page 80).

2 ripe avocados, halved and seeded

1/2 cup (120 ml) fresh orange juice

2 cloves garlic, smashed and very finely chopped

1/2 teaspoon kosher or sea salt

1/4 teaspoon ground black pepper

1 tablespoon fruity extra virgin olive oil

1/4 teaspoon dried orange peel

1/2 cup (90 g) pomegranate arils

1/4 cup (10 g) finely chopped fresh parsley leaves

Scoop out the flesh from the avocados with a soup spoon and mash, with a fork or manual masher (Basic Mashing Tools, page 10), in a medium bowl with the orange juice, garlic, salt, and pepper. Fold in the olive oil, orange peel, pomegranate arils, and fresh parsley. Serve immediately or tightly wrap (to the surface of the guacamole) with plastic wrap and serve within the hour. Garnish with a few more pomegranate seeds and fresh parsley.

THYME, TURNIP, AND FIJI APPLE MASH

YIELDS 6 TO 8 SERVINGS

Earthy turnips get a sweet, acidic edge from Fiji apples in this simple, elegant side, and the lemon kick from fragrant thyme is the perfect counter. Add a bit more of the flavorful turnip cooking liquid to transform this into a lovely soup. As a mash or as a soup, these flavors pair beautifully with roasted chicken or pork.

6 medium turnips, peeled and cut into 2-inch (5-cm) cubes

1 shallot, peeled and quartered

2 cups (475 ml) low-sodium vegetable stock

1 cup (240 ml) water

3 sprigs fresh thyme

1 teaspoon kosher or sea salt

1/2 teaspoon ground black pepper

1 large Fiji apple, cored and cut into 2-inch (5-cm) cubes

2 tablespoons finely chopped fresh thyme leaves

2 tablespoons unsalted butter

1 tablespoon honey

1 tablespoon full-fat sour cream

Kosher or sea salt and ground black pepper, to taste

Place the turnips, shallot, stock, water, thyme branches, salt, and pepper in a large saucepan. Bring to a boil over high heat and reduce to a simmer over medium to medium low. Cook, uncovered, for 10 minutes. Add the apple and cook for another 15–20 minutes, until both the turnips and apple easily yield and crumble when pierced with a fork or knife.

Remove from the heat and discard the thyme branches. Strain in a colander over a large bowl and reserve the cooking liquid separately; you will have about 2 cups (475 ml). Place the strained turnips in the bowl of a food processor fitted with a metal blade. Stream in 3/4 cup (356 ml) of the reserved cooking liquid into the machine while running and process until the mixture is light and fluffy. Add fresh thyme, butter, honey, and sour cream. Pulse until incorporated. You can also do the mashing using a manual masher (Basic Mashing Tools, page 10) in the cooking pot or a large bowl. Taste and adjust seasonings as needed. Serve hot. Can be made ahead, refrigerated, and reheated over low heat or a water bath before serving.

BUTTERNUT-BABY KALE SHELLS AND CHEESE BAKE

YIELDS 8 TO 10 SERVINGS

Roasted and puréed butternut squash is fortified with sautéed baby kale and plenty of cheddar cheese in this grown up version of mac 'n' cheese that will keep even the kids coming back for more.

1 medium butternut squash

SHELLS
Water

3 tablespoons kosher or sea salt

1/2 pound (3 cups / 230 g) medium pasta shells

KALE
2 tablespoons olive oil

1 medium shallot, finely chopped

2 cloves garlic, finely chopped

Pinch of kosher or sea salt and ground black pepper

6 cups (95 g) coarsely chopped baby kale leaves or lacinato kale leaves

1/2 teaspoon apple cider vinegar

1/8 teaspoon ground nutmeg

BÉCHAMEL AND FINISHING
5 tablespoons unsalted butter, divided

3 tablespoons all-purpose flour

4 cups (950 ml) half-and-half

1 cup (120 g) full-fat ricotta cheese

1 tablespoon kosher or sea salt

2 teaspoons ground black pepper

1/2 teaspoon ground nutmeg

1/2 cup (90 g) grated Parmesan cheese

Preheat oven to 425° F (220° C). Cut squash in half, remove seeds, and place, cut side down, on a baking sheet. Roast for 45 minutes, or until very soft. Remove from oven and set aside. Reduce oven temperature to 350° F (175° C).

SHELLS Bring a large pot of water to a boil with the salt. Add shells and cook al dente, about 8 minutes. Drain and set aside.

KALE In a large saucepan, heat the oil over medium heat. Add the shallot, garlic, and salt and pepper; cook until just softened, about 5 minutes. Add kale and stir to coat. Cook, stirring until completely wilted, about 5 minutes. Add vinegar and nutmeg, stir, and set aside.

BÉCHAMEL AND FINISHING Melt 3 tablespoons butter over medium heat in a large pot. Whisk in flour and cook for 2 minutes. Whisk in half-and-half and stir at a low simmer for 3 minutes. Scoop the flesh away from the skin of the cooked squash and into the simmering béchamel. Whisk thoroughly to combine, or if necessary, blend until smooth with an immersion blender (Basic Mashing Tools, page 10). Whisk in the ricotta, salt, pepper, nutmeg, and 1 tablespoon of butter. Fold in the cooked shells.

Butter a large shallow casserole dish with the remaining butter. Pour in the pasta mixture and spread evenly. Sprinkle the Parmesan evenly over the top. Bake until bubbling hot and lightly browned, 40 minutes. Serve hot. Leftovers will heat well in a 350° F (175° C) oven or in a microwave.

CHEDDAR-POTATO CHIP CRUNCH BROCCOLI GRATIN

YIELDS 8 SERVINGS

Another quintessential comfort food classic, this one will find favor with kids and adults alike. An old-school potato chip (preferably Lay's Classic) crunch on top seals the deal on the cheesy broccoli center, making this a soul-and-belly-warming hit on a cold winter's night.

Water

3 tablespoons kosher or sea salt

1 large head broccoli, stalks removed and broken into florets

BÉCHAMEL AND FINISHING

3 tablespoons unsalted butter, divided

1 tablespoon finely chopped shallot

Pinch of kosher or sea salt and ground black pepper

2 tablespoons all-purpose flour

1 1/2 cups (350 ml) half-and-half or whole milk

3/4 cup (180 ml) buttermilk

1 teaspoon kosher or sea salt

1/2 teaspoon ground black pepper

1/4 cup (10 g) finely chopped chives

Pinch of crushed red pepper

2 cups (240 g) grated mild cheddar cheese

1 egg, beaten

1 cup (35 g) crushed potato chips

Preheat oven to 350° F (175° C). Bring a large pot of water to a rolling boil with the salt and add the broccoli. Parboil for 3 minutes. Pour out into a colander and rinse with cold water, tossing, for 3 minutes to set the color and stop the cooking. Set aside.

BÉCHAMEL AND FINISHING Meanwhile, melt 2 tablespoons butter over medium heat in a large pot. Add the shallot, salt, and pepper; stir together and cook until softened, about 3 minutes. Add the flour, stir, and cook for another 2 minutes. Add the half-and-half and buttermilk, whisking the whole time, and bring to a simmer over medium-high heat. Cook for 3–5 minutes. Remove from heat and stir in the reserved broccoli.

Mash with an immersion blender (Basic Mashing Tools, page 10), pressing down on the tops of the florets to lightly break them up. Stir in salt, pepper, chives, crushed red pepper, cheese, and the egg.

Butter a large deep casserole dish with the remaining butter. Pour in the mixture and top with an even layer of the crushed potato chips. Bake for 60 minutes, until bubbling and golden. Let rest at room temperature for 10 minutes. Serve very hot. Leftovers will heat well in a 350° F (175° C) oven. Microwaving will muddle the crunch of the crust.

BUTTERY BRUSSELS SPROUT MASH

YIELDS 4 TO 6 SERVINGS

A bright splash of fresh lemon and plenty of butter give this humble sprout a dash of pluck and panache that would be extra delicious paired with a mild, milky fish like sole or grouper.

1 pound (450 g) fresh Brussels sprouts, trimmed and cut into roughly equal sizes (halved or quartered)

1 small shallot, peeled and quartered

1 cup (240 ml) low-sodium chicken stock

1 teaspoon kosher or sea salt

1/2 teaspoon ground black pepper

2 tablespoons unsalted butter

Juice of 1/2 lemon (about 2 tablespoons)

1 tablespoon half-and-half

Place the Brussels sprouts in a medium pot with the shallot, stock, salt, and pepper. Bring to a boil over high heat, reduce to a simmer over medium and cook for 35–40 minutes, uncovered, until very tender. Place the sprouts, shallot, and all of the cooking liquid in a food processor fitted with a metal blade. Purée until smooth. Pulse in the butter, lemon juice, and half-and-half. Serve hot with a pat of butter melting on the top. Reheats very well in the microwave or over a water bath.

SPRING

MINTY SPRING PEA LETTUCE WRAPS

Fresh spring peas are simmered in water with fresh mint and puréed until silky smooth in their fragrant cooking liquid. The emerald-toned purée is chilled and wrapped in buttery Bibb lettuce and topped with crunchy fresh radishes, making a beautiful, delicious, and purely spring presentation.

4 cups (600 g) fresh or frozen peas

2 cups (475 ml) low-sodium vegetable stock

¹/₄ cup (10 g) fresh mint leaves

¹/₂ teaspoon kosher or sea salt

¹/₄ teaspoon ground black pepper

12 to 14 leaves Bibb lettuce (or another butterhead lettuce variety)

6 radishes, trimmed, washed, and very finely sliced

Place the peas in a medium pot with the stock, mint, salt, and pepper. Bring to a boil over high heat; reduce to a simmer over medium low, and cook, uncovered, for 20 minutes.

Strain the peas through a colander over a large bowl, reserving the cooking liquid. In the bowl of a food processor fitted with a metal blade, purée the peas with 1 cup (240 ml) of the cooking liquid, or aggressively mash the same ingredients together in a large bowl with a manual masher (Basic Mashing Tools, page 10), adding the liquid in increments. Taste and adjust seasoning as needed. Refrigerate for several hours or overnight.

To compile the wraps, place a generous dollop of the purée in the center of a lettuce leaf, top with 3 or 4 radish slices, and wrap the lettuce around the filling to form a tube. Chill until ready to serve. Serve on a platter garnished with fresh mint, if desired.

GINGER AND CUMIN-SPICED CARROT MASH

YIELDS 6 TO 8 SERVINGS

Sweet spring carrots get roasted then take a swim with fresh ginger-infused coconut milk in this brilliantly colored cumin-enhanced mash that is lovely as a side to roast chicken.

2 pounds (900 g) carrots, peeled and cut into 2-inch (5-cm) lengths

2 tablespoons olive oil

2 tablespoons kosher or sea salt

1 teaspoon ground black pepper

2 cups (475 ml) coconut milk

8 thin slices peeled fresh ginger

1 teaspoon ground cumin

1 teaspoon ground ginger

1 teaspoon kosher or sea salt

⅓ cup (75 g) full-fat sour cream

2 tablespoons unsalted butter

2 scallions, trimmed and coarsely chopped

Preheat oven to 425° F (220° C). Toss the carrots with the olive oil, 2 tablespoons salt, and pepper on a baking sheet and arrange in a single layer. Roast for 40 minutes, tossing once halfway through cooking, until the carrots are very soft and lightly browned. Remove from the oven and set aside.

Simmer the coconut milk with the fresh ginger in a small saucepan for 40 minutes, while the carrots are roasting. Remove the fresh ginger and discard. Add the cumin, ground ginger, and 1 teaspoon salt to the coconut milk. Place the carrots in the bowl of a food processor fitted with a metal blade. Stream the warm coconut milk into the carrots while the machine is running. Process until very smooth. If using a manual masher (Basic Mashing Tools, page 10), stream the coconut milk into the bowl while mashing. Add the sour cream, butter, and scallions and pulse to combine, or stir into the pot while finishing the manual mash. Serve hot.

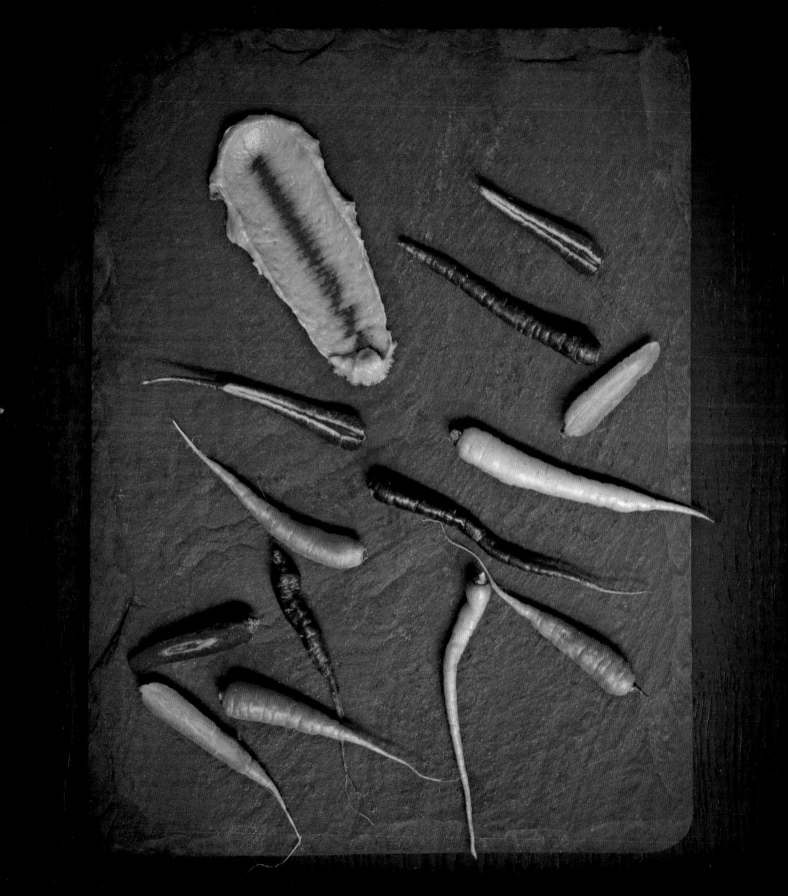

ROASTED BEET AND SOUR CREAM DILL MASH

YIELDS 4 TO 6 SERVINGS

Beets are available in a rainbow of colors these days, but I love the way roasting brings out the deep royal-purple tones of the traditional purple variety used here. Dill and sour cream recall borscht, but this is a beautiful thick purée perfectly befitting a bright spring table.

8 medium beets, scrubbed and halved (or cut into nearly equal pieces)
1 tablespoon olive oil
1 tablespoon balsamic vinegar
Generous pinch of kosher or sea salt and ground black pepper
1/2 cup (115 g) full-fat sour cream
1/4 cup (2 g) chopped fresh dill fronds
1/4 cup (60 ml) water
3/4 teaspoon kosher or sea salt
1/2 teaspoon ground black pepper

Preheat oven to 425° F (220° C). Toss the beets with the olive oil, vinegar, salt, and pepper on a baking sheet. Arrange, cut side down, and roast for 60 minutes, or until softened. Remove from oven and allow to cool until easily handled but still warm. Peel the skins off the beets, using a paring knife, and discard.

In a food processor fitted with a metal blade, purée warm beets with the sour cream, dill, water, salt, and pepper until chunky smooth, or mash the whole mixture together in a large bowl using a manual masher (Basic Mashing Tools, page 10). Serve hot with a sprinkle of freshly chopped dill, if desired.

CREAMED ONION SOUP

One of the most exciting sights of spring is seeing tender new spears break through the still chilly earth, and of those fresh new spears, onions are undoubtedly my favorite. Sweet, fresh spring onions are the backbone to this gloriously delicate soup. Choose the very white onions with the green tops at your grocery store or farmers market. Off season, regular yellow onions will work fine.

3 tablespoons unsalted butter

6 medium spring onions, trimmed, halved, and thinly sliced (peel any tough or dried skin)

1 tablespoon plus 1 1/2 teaspoons kosher or sea salt, divided

1 1/2 teaspoons ground pepper, divided

1 tablespoon sweet vermouth

1 tablespoon all-purpose flour

1/2 cup (120 ml) half-and-half

1 cup water, if needed

Melt the butter in a large pot over medium heat. Add the onions, 1 tablespoon salt, and 1 teaspoon pepper. Stir to coat. Cook over medium-low heat for 30–40 minutes, until softened and wilted. Add the vermouth and cook through, about 1 minute. Add the flour and stir to coat, cooking for 1 minute. Add the remaining salt, remaining pepper, and the half-and-half. Cook together for 5 minutes. Purée in the pot with an immersion blender (Basic Mashing Tools, page 10) until smooth and frothy. Add water or additional cream and adjust seasoning, if needed.

EGGS, FISH,
MEAT, GRAINS
& LEGUMES

Although they're not as commonly thought of as mash appropriate as their potato and vegetable counterparts, eggs, fish, meat, grains (in this chapter we use quinoa, which is technically a seed), and especially legumes are very much great mash candidates. Whether dried, soaked overnight, or canned, all legumes break down into beautiful mashes that invite myriad, globally inspired flavor pairings. Depending on the type of bean and whether dried, canned, or frozen, the texture results and cooking time vary considerably.

Some of the shining legume stars in this chapter include Creamed Spinach and Ham Lentil Soup (page 133), Delicate Lemon-Thyme Hummus (page 134), Spicy Red Lentil and Carrot Soup (page 137), and a Mexican Black Bean Nacho Bake (page 130). These descriptions alone will give you a sense of the wonderful diversity of the humble, nutritious, and delicious legume. Meats gets mashed with a Chunky Chicken Liver Pâté and an elegant Dried Cherry and Orange Compote (page 124), seeds are folded into tasty mashed cauliflower in the Lemony Quinoa and Cauliflower Mash (page 126), and you'll simply never taste a better egg salad than the Chunky Egg Salad and Caper Mash (page 129).

SOUTHERN-STYLE SHRIMP AND SCALLION PASTE SANDWICHES

YIELDS 2 CUPS OR ABOUT 32 TEA SANDWICHES

In the South, a region I've called home for over nearly two decades, shrimp and good manners are ridiculously abundant. Perhaps that is why these briny, delicate sandwiches are standard to the point of almost required fare at most cocktail and tea parties in Charleston. There is a celebrated caterer here who has all but built her stellar reputation on them. Buy the shrimp with their shells on. They add flavor to the fumet that is processed back into the shrimp spread.

1 tablespoon unsalted butter

1 small shallot, finely chopped

Pinch of kosher or sea salt and ground pepper

3/4 pound (340 g) 16 to 20 count shrimp (12 to 16 shrimp), shells on and well rinsed

1/2 cup (120 ml) good-quality Chardonnay

1 stick (1/2 cup / 115 g) unsalted butter

4 scallions, green and white parts, root and tips trimmed

1/2 teaspoon kosher or sea salt

1/2 teaspoon ground black pepper

16 slices soft white bread (optional)

Melt 1 tablespoon butter in a medium saucepan over medium heat. Add the shallot, salt, and pepper. Stir to coat and continue cooking for another 5 minutes, or until the shallots are soft and translucent. Add the shrimp and Chardonnay and increase heat to medium high. Cook, stirring, until the shrimp are opaque and pale pink. Remove the shrimp with a slotted spoon and set aside.

Reduce the cooking liquid to 3 tablespoons, cooking over high heat. Add the stick of butter to the pan, melt over medium heat, and set aside.

Peel and devein the shrimp (page 13), carefully rinsing to remove all parts of the grainy central vein. Place the shrimp and scallions in the bowl of a food processor fitted with a metal blade. Process, streaming in the reserved warm butter mixture while running. Add salt and pepper. Chill, covered, for 3 hours to overnight.

Serve at room temperature as a dip for crudité or as a filling for delicate tea sandwiches, using about 1/4 cup (60 g) to fill each sandwich, removing crusts after filling, and cutting into 4 triangles for each sandwich. Keep the bread moist by covering with a damp paper towel and wrapping tightly with plastic wrap until just before serving.

CHUNKY CHICKEN LIVER PÂTÉ WITH DRIED CHERRY AND ORANGE COMPOTE

EACH RECIPE YIELDS 2 CUPS (400 G)

When properly prepared, chicken liver pâté (or the poor man's foie gras) is hardly discernible from its posh pâté cousin and costs pennies, opposed to hundreds, to prepare. While often combined with dried prunes macerated in cognac (which is delicious), the liver's mellow, slightly sweet flavor and texture meets its match in a lively, festive dried cherry and fresh orange juice compote. Spread some pâté on the Baguette Crostini (facing page) and dip or top with a thin room-temperature layer of the compote. The colors are exquisite and perfectly suited to budget-friendly holiday entertaining.

PÂTÉ

5 tablespoons unsalted butter, divided

1 medium onion, finely chopped
(about 1 1/2 cups / 230 g)

1 pound (450 g) chicken livers,
coarsely chopped

1 tablespoon chopped fresh thyme
leaves

1 teaspoon kosher or sea salt

1/2 teaspoon ground black pepper

2 tablespoons cognac or brandy

COMPOTE

1 small shallot, finely chopped

1 cup (160 g) coarsely chopped
dried tart cherries

1 cup (240 ml) Merlot

3 sprigs fresh thyme

Pinch of kosher or sea salt

1 cup (240 ml) fresh orange juice
(do not substitute processed or
concentrated)

1 teaspoon fresh lemon zest

1/8 teaspoon ground cloves

PÂTÉ Melt 2 tablespoons butter in a large skillet over medium-low heat. Add the onion and cook, stirring, until very soft, about 10 minutes. Add the chicken livers, thyme, salt, and pepper. Stir and cook for 5 minutes, or until the livers are nearly cooked through. Add the cognac and remaining butter. Increase heat to medium high. Cook for another 1–2 minutes, or until the liver is a very pale pink in the center and grayish on the exterior. Remove from heat and place in the bowl of a food processor fitted with a metal blade. Process 10 times, or until the pâté is chunky smooth. Refrigerate, covered, for 3 hours to overnight. Serve at room temperature.

COMPOTE Place the shallot, cherries, Merlot, thyme, and salt in a small saucepan. Bring to a boil over high heat and reduce by half, about 4–5 minutes. Add the orange juice, lemon zest, and cloves. Bring to a simmer over medium heat and cook, uncovered, until the liquid has reduced to 1/4 cup (60 ml) and the cherries are soft and breaking apart, about 20 minutes. Remove from heat. Discard the thyme. Mash with a manual masher (Basic Mashing Tools, page 10) until coarsely smashed and puréed. Refrigerate, covered, for 3 hours to overnight. Serve at room temperature.

BAGUETTE CROSTINI

32 TOAST POINTS

Crostini are toasted points of bread. For me, the best bread candidate is a day-old white-bread French baguette. Slightly less-fresh bread will soak up more of the olive oil and seasoning flavors that will seep into it while it's toasting in a hot oven. You can rub it down with a smashed clove of garlic, if desired, for some of the other dip recipes in this chapter, but I don't recommend doing that if using for the Chicken Liver Pâté with Dried Cherry and Orange Compote (facing page). Once fully cooled, store in an air tight container for up to 1 day. Re-crisp in a hot oven for 1–2 minutes before serving.

1 day-old white French baguette
2 to 3 tablespoons extra virgin olive oil
1/2 teaspoon kosher or sea salt
1/2 teaspoon ground black pepper

Preheat oven to 425° F (220° C). Cut the bread on the diagonal into 1/4-inch (6-mm) slices and place on a baking sheet with the remaining ingredients. Toss with your hands to evenly coat the bread. Arrange in a single layer on the sheet (using 2 sheets if necessary) and place in the oven. After 10 minutes, or as the toasts are just becoming golden, turn using a spatula. Toast for another 2 minutes. Remove from oven and cool on paper towels.

LEMONY QUINOA AND CAULIFLOWER MASH

YIELDS 8 TO 10 SERVINGS

Steamed cauliflower mashed with fresh lemon juice and a scant amount of sour cream folds like blankets of snow around pop-when-you-bite-them quinoa seeds. Refreshing and light, this recipe is also gluten free, vegetarian, and with the omission of the small amounts of sour cream and butter, vegan. If your definition of delicious doesn't necessarily go with healthy, this recipe will change your mind forever.

1 cup (170 g) quinoa

2 cups (475 ml) water

Pinch of kosher or sea salt

1 medium head cauliflower, quartered and cut into small florets

1 cup (240 ml) low-sodium chicken stock

1 3/4 teaspoons kosher or sea salt, divided

Juice from 1/2 lemon (about 2 tablespoons)

2 tablespoons unsalted butter

1/2 cup (115 g) full-fat sour cream

3/4 teaspoon ground black pepper

1/3 cup (15 g) finely chopped fresh parsley leaves

Place the quinoa, water, and pinch of salt in a medium saucepan and bring to a boil over high heat. Reduce to a simmer over medium-low heat and cook, covered, for 10–15 minutes, until all of the water has been absorbed by the quinoa. Fluff with a fork and set aside, uncovered.

Meanwhile, place the cauliflower florets in a medium saucepan with the stock and 1 teaspoon salt. Bring to a boil over high heat, reduce to a simmer over medium low, cover, and cook for 10 minutes, or until the florets break easily when pierced with a fork or knife.

Drain off all but 1/4 cup (60 ml) of the cooking liquid. Using a manual masher (Basic Mashing Tools, page 10), mash in the same pan with lemon juice, butter, sour cream, remaining salt, and pepper until smooth. Fold in the quinoa and fresh parsley using a spatula. Serve warm or at room temperature. Refrigerate, covered, for up to 1 day before serving.

CHUNKY EGG SALAD AND CAPER MASH

YIELDS 2¹/₂ CUPS (500 G) OR 8 SERVINGS

A good old-fashioned manual mash merges perfectly cooked boiled eggs with the perky flavors of capers, fresh herbs, celery, and red onion. Barely bound with sour cream and mayo, it's exceptionally light, bright, and delicious. Serve it as an egg salad on a bed of greens or as part of a composed salad, or on soft white bread for sandwiches (about ¹/₄ cup / 50 g per sandwich) with a thin layer of mild, crisp lettuce. It's also very refreshing served in hollowed lengths of well-drained cucumber boats for summer entertaining and party presentation.

8 large eggs, room temperature
Water
1 tablespoon apple cider vinegar
¹/₄ cup (60 g) full-fat sour cream
¹/₄ cup (55 g) mayonnaise
2 teaspoons Dijon mustard
¹/₄ cup (40 g) very finely chopped red onion
¹/₄ cup (25 g) very finely chopped celery
1 tablespoon finely chopped fresh thyme leaves
1 tablespoon drained and coarsely chopped capers
1 teaspoon caper brine
¹/₂ teaspoon kosher or sea salt
¹/₂ teaspoon ground black pepper

Gently place the eggs in a medium pot. Cover generously with water (at least 2 inches / 5 cm above the eggs) and add the vinegar. Bring to a boil over high heat. Once at a full boil, remove from heat and keep the eggs in the heated water for exactly 15 minutes. Drain. Place the eggs in a bowl of heavily iced cold water for exactly 5 minutes. Drain.

Peel and remove the shell of each egg under running tap water. Cut each egg into thirds, horizontally. Place in a medium bowl and mash with a manual masher (Basic Mashing Tools, page 10) until light and fluffy, all yolks and whites evenly broken. Add remaining ingredients and stir to combine with a spatula. Chill, covered, for at least 1 hour or overnight.

MEXICAN BLACK BEAN NACHO BAKE

YIELDS 8 TO 10 SERVINGS

A bit of help using canned black beans, tortilla chips, queso sauce, and salsa from your grocer's shelves brings this filling, crunchy, cheesy, spicy casserole of Mexican goodness together in fairly short order. It's perfect for game day or any time you've got a hungry crowd on your hands.

3 tablespoons olive oil

1 poblano chile pepper, seeded and finely diced

1 jalapeño pepper, seeded and finely diced

1/2 red onion, peeled and finely diced

1 stalk celery, finely diced

1 teaspoon kosher or sea salt

1/2 teaspoon ground black pepper

2 teaspoons ground cumin

1 teaspoon dried oregano leaves

4 large cloves garlic, peeled, smashed, and finely diced

2 (15.5-ounce / 440-g) cans black beans, well-drained

1 teaspoon red wine vinegar

1 cup (260 g) medium tomato salsa

1/2 cup (120 ml) low-sodium chicken stock

1 tablespoon coarsely chopped unsweetened 90 percent dark chocolate

1 tablespoon honey

1 tablespoon unsalted butter

2 cups (240 g) grated sharp cheddar cheese, divided

2 cups (126 g) crushed corn tortilla chips

1 1/2 cups (180 g) queso cheese

Preheat oven to 325° F (160° C). Heat the olive oil over medium heat in a large saucepan. Add the poblano, jalapeño, onion, celery, salt, pepper, cumin, oregano, and garlic; stir to coat. Cook for 5 minutes over medium heat, until softened. Add the black beans, vinegar, salsa, and stock. Stir then simmer over medium heat, uncovered, for 15 minutes. Add the chocolate and honey. Continue to simmer for 10–15 minutes.

Using a manual masher (Basic Mashing Tools, page 10), mash until chunky smooth. Taste and adjust seasoning as needed.

Grease a 2-quart (2-l) casserole dish with the butter. Using a spatula, evenly spread the black bean mixture into the casserole. Top with 1 cup (120 g) cheddar cheese. Top this with the crushed tortilla chips, and then top with the remaining cheddar cheese. Bake, uncovered, for 10 minutes. Remove from oven and top with an even layer of queso cheese. Bake for another 20 minutes. Serve hot, fresh from the oven, with a dollop of sour cream and additional salsa or queso, if desired.

CREAMED SPINACH AND HAM LENTIL SOUP

Of all the lentil varieties available these days, French green lentils are undeniably my favorite. Here they get a little flavor help from smoked ham. Exotic spices like allspice and nutmeg give it Moroccan warmth, which is welcome on a chilly day. Be judicious with salt, adding it only near the end, as the ham contains a good amount of it.

4 tablespoons unsalted butter, divided

1 tablespoon olive oil

1¼ pound (565 g) cooked smoked ham steak, cut into small cubes

2 teaspoons ground black pepper, divided

2 teaspoons ground allspice, divided

1½ teaspoons ground nutmeg, divided

1 large leek, white and pale-green parts only, cut into medium dice

2 large cloves garlic, minced

1 stalk celery, cut into medium dice

1 shallot, cut into medium dice

1 teaspoon kosher or sea salt

1 cup (240 ml) red wine, such as Merlot or Cabernet Sauvignon

2 cups (400 g) dried French green lentils

6 cups (1,400 ml) low-sodium chicken stock

2 bay leaves

2 cups (475 ml) water, as needed

2 cups (310) thawed frozen chopped spinach

½ cup (120 ml) half-and-half

1 teaspoon red wine vinegar

Melt the olive oil and 2 tablespoons butter in a large soup pot over medium-high heat. Add the ham and stir to coat. Add 1 teaspoon pepper, 1 teaspoon allspice, and ½ teaspoon nutmeg. Increase heat to high. Continue cooking, uncovered, stirring until the ham starts giving off its juices and begins to turn a golden brown, about 10 minutes. Remove the ham from the pot with a slotted spoon and set aside.

Add remaining butter to the same cooking pot and melt over medium heat. Add the leek, garlic, celery, and shallot. Cook over medium heat, stirring, until softened, about 5 minutes. Add remaining pepper, nutmeg, allspice, and salt. Add the wine, cooking over high heat, and reduce to a glaze. Add the lentils, stock, and bay leaves. Bring to a boil over high, reduce to a simmer over medium low, and cook for 40 minutes, uncovered, until the lentils are tender but still hold their shape. Add additional water as needed. You're looking for a soup-like consistency.

Remove bay leaves and discard. Add the spinach and simmer, stirring until wilted and heated through, about 10 minutes. Mash with an immersion blender (Basic Mashing Tools, page 10) until the soup is chunky smooth but most lentils still retain their shape. Return the ham to the pot and heat over medium. Finish with the half-and-half and vinegar. Taste and adjust seasonings as needed. Leftovers will store well refrigerated for a few days, but may continue absorbing liquid. Add more liquid as needed when reheating.

DELICATE LEMON-THYME HUMMUS

YIELDS 2 CUPS (500 G)

Hummus originated in the Middle East, but its popularity has spread to cultures throughout the world. This fluffy garbanzo bean (also called chickpea) purée gets texture levity from a food processor, but they could be mashed manually for a chunkier effect. Fresh lemon and thyme deliver a pop of freshness. This is where you want to use the fruitiest best-quality extra virgin olive oil you can find—ideally, first press. Serve room temperature with Homemade Pita Chips (page 80) or Baguette Crostini (page 125).

1 (15.5-ounce / 440-g) can garbanzo beans, drained

2 large cloves garlic, smashed and coarsely chopped

Juice of 1 large lemon (about $1/2$ cup / 120 ml)

3 tablespoons tahini

$1/2$ to $3/4$ cup (120 to 180 ml) extra virgin olive oil

1 teaspoon kosher or sea salt

$1/2$ teaspoon ground black pepper

$1/3$ cup (12 g) fresh thyme leaves

GARNISH

Additional extra virgin olive oil (about $1/4$ cup / 60 ml)

$1/4$ teaspoon paprika

3 or 4 sprigs fresh thyme

Place the garbanzo beans, garlic, lemon, and tahini in the bowl of a food processor fitted with a metal blade. Process until smooth—it will be thick and start to form a ball. Stream in $1/2$ to $3/4$ cup (120 to 180 ml) olive oil while the processor is running. The consistency will be fluffy and light. Pulse (10 brief pulses) and add in salt, pepper, and fresh thyme, scraping down the sides with a spatula to incorporate. Serve in a shallow bowl or platter, spread evenly with a small pool in the center. Pour in additional olive oil garnish, sprinkle with paprika, and garnish with fresh thyme.

SPICY RED LENTIL AND CARROT SOUP

MAKES 6 TO 8 SERVINGS

Chunks of sweet carrot lightly mashed into the beautiful red (really a deep orange) lentil purée make for a stunning presentation. Cumin and chipotle add just the right amount of heat, countered with fresh mint and scallion garnish. Unlike the French lentils, these pulpy legumes purée as they cook in very little time, making this an exceptionally fast and easy soup in contrast to its showstopping appearance and taste.

1 tablespoon unsalted butter

1 tablespoon olive oil

1 shallot, finely chopped

2 large cloves garlic, smashed and chopped

2 large carrots, peeled and cut into 1/8-inch (3-mm) coins (about 2 cups / 260 g)

1 teaspoon kosher or sea salt

1/2 teaspoon ground black pepper

2 teaspoons ground cumin

1 teaspoon ground smoked chipotle

Pinch of crushed red pepper

2 cups (400 g) red lentils

6 cups (1,400 ml) low-sodium vegetable stock

1 tablespoon finely chopped fresh mint leaves

2 scallions, green and white parts, trimmed and finely chopped

Melt the butter and oil together over medium heat in a large saucepan. Add the shallot, garlic, carrots, salt, pepper, cumin, chipotle, and crushed red pepper. Stir and sauté together to soften and incorporate the spices, about 5 minutes.

Add the lentils and stock. Bring to a boil over high heat and reduce to a simmer over medium-low heat. Cook for 15–20 minutes, until lentils have cooked to a pulp and the carrots are very soft. Mash briefly with a manual masher (Basic Mashing Tools, page 10) in the cooking pot to break the carrots into small chunks. Return to heat and bring to a simmer. Serve hot with a sprinkle of fresh mint and scallions in each bowl. Will store beautifully refrigerated for a few days, but leave the garnishes separate from the soup until service.

CITRUS CANNELLINI BEAN AND RAINBOW CHARD MASH

YIELDS 6 TO 8 SERVINGS

Buttery, mild canned cannellini beans come home to Italy with bright flavors of lemon and orange and are topped with a colorful mound of rainbow chard to finish. Reminiscent of spring, this is another beautiful vegetarian dish that can be served all year long.

CHARD

3 tablespoons olive oil

1/2 medium red onion, finely diced

3 cloves garlic, smashed and finely diced

1 bunch fresh rainbow chard, well washed and dried, tough stalks removed, and cut into a chiffonade (page 12) (about 6 cups / 215 g)

1 teaspoon kosher or sea salt

1/2 teaspoon ground black pepper

1 teaspoon red wine vinegar

BEANS

2 (15.5-ounce / 440-g) cans cannellini beans, drained

1/4 cup (60 ml) fresh lemon juice

1/4 cup (60 ml) fresh orange juice

1 tablespoon extra virgin olive oil

1 teaspoon kosher or sea salt

1/2 teaspoon ground black pepper

CHARD Heat the olive oil over medium heat in a large sauté pan. Add the onion and garlic and cook until softened, about 5 minutes. Add the chard and season with salt and pepper. Stir to coat. The chard will very quickly wilt down to just a cup or so of cooked greens. Drizzle the vinegar over the greens, stir, and continue to cook, for 7–8 minutes, until all of the liquid has evaporated from the pan.

BEANS In a medium saucepan, mash the beans with the lemon juice, orange juice, olive oil, salt, and pepper using a manual masher (Basic Mashing Tools, page 10) until chunky smooth. Heat over medium-low heat, stirring, until the bean mixture is warm. Serve the hot greens over (or under) a mound of warm beans. Both components will store well refrigerated, but store in separate covered containers and reheat separately before serving.

LUMP CRAB BRANDADE

Brandade is a French Provençal staple, typically prepared with salt cod. Because cod can be hard to find and is slightly less elegant, I substituted sweet lump crab meat for it in this recipe. The mashed potatoes bake with the crab and plenty of olive oil and garlic for a fluffy, satisfying side that is equally at home spread warm on crostini (Baguette Crostini, page 80) and drizzled with extra virgin olive oil and fresh thyme. Add a salad and you've got a beautiful meal.

3 medium russet potatoes, peeled and cut into 1-inch (2.5-cm) cubes

3 cloves garlic, smashed

1 medium shallot, peeled and cut into 6 pieces

Water

2 teaspoons salt

4 sprigs fresh thyme

1 tablespoon finely chopped fresh thyme leaves

2 tablespoons fresh lemon juice

1/2 cup (115 g) full-fat sour cream

3 tablespoons extra virgin olive oil

1/2 cup (120 ml) half-and-half

1/2 teaspoon ground black pepper

1/2 teaspoon ground smoked chipotle

8 ounces (230 g) cooked lump crab meat

1 tablespoon unsalted butter, room temperature

Extra virgin olive oil

Fresh thyme sprigs

Preheat oven to 350° F (175° C). Place the potatoes, garlic, and shallot in a medium saucepan. Cover with water. Add salt and thyme sprigs, bring to a boil over high, reduce to a simmer over medium low, and cook, uncovered, until the potatoes are tender, 15–20 minutes. Drain well and discard thyme. Return the rest to the same cooking pot.

Add fresh thyme leaves, lemon juice, sour cream, olive oil, half-and-half, pepper, and chipotle. Mash with manual masher (Basic Mashing Tools, page 10) until smooth and incorporated. Carefully fold in the crab meat with a spatula, being gentle to not break up the crab.

Butter a 1½-quart (1.5-l) casserole dish with the butter and spoon the mixture into the casserole dish. Bake at 350° F (175° C) for 50 minutes to 1 hour, until fluffy and lightly golden on top. Serve warm, garnished with olive oil and thyme springs, as a side dish or crostini spread.

LUCKY PROSPERITY SOUP

YIELDS 8 TO 10 SERVINGS

New Year's Day in the South ushers in a call to wealth and prosperity, which are symbolized by black-eyed peas (representing coins) and collard greens (representing greenbacks). Often, they're cooked separately, usually with some ham hock for flavor, and put together on the same plate with rice. This delicious soup takes the best of the bunch and puts them all in one pot, with the exclusion of rice. If you can't find collard greens, substitute kale or another sturdy green. This soup is finished with a traditional sweet and onion splash from a southern garnish known as chow-chow. If you cannot find it, substitute a traditional relish, but modify the results as suggested in the recipe.

1 tablespoon unsalted butter

1 tablespoon olive oil

1 medium onion, finely chopped

2 stalks celery, finely chopped

2 cloves garlic, smashed and diced

3 teaspoons kosher or sea salt, divided

1 1/2 teaspoons ground black pepper

1 tablespoon red wine vinegar

4 cups (1 1/4 pounds / 565 g) rehydrated black-eyed peas, rinsed

3/4 pound (340 g) smoked ham hock

8 cups (1,9 l) water

1 large bunch collard greens, rinsed, tough stems removed and discarded, and cut into 1/4-inch (6-mm) strips

1 teaspoon hot pepper sauce or Tabasco

1/3 cup (80 g) chow-chow or 2 tablespoons traditional relish

Melt the butter with the olive oil in a large soup pot or Dutch oven over medium heat. Add the onion, celery, garlic, 1 teaspoon salt, and 1/2 teaspoon pepper. Stir to coat. Cook until the vegetables have softened, about 5 minutes. Deglaze with the vinegar and reduce quickly to a glaze.

Add the peas, ham, water, collard greens, and remaining salt and pepper. Bring to a boil over high and reduce to a simmer. Cook, uncovered, for 1 hour, until thickened and the greens have cooked down and the peas are soft but holding their shape. Remove the ham hock from the pot and set aside to cool.

Meanwhile, using an immersion blender (Basic Mashing Tools, page 10), briefly mash the soup in the cooking pot to help incorporate the beans and the greens. When cool enough to handle, cut off and remove outer fat and skin layer from the hock. Cut off any visible meat, finely chop, and return to the pot; discard the rest. Just before serving, stir in the hot sauce and chow-chow. Adjust salt and pepper as needed. Serve steaming hot and sit back and count your lucky stars.

BACON-BLESSED BAKED BEANS

YIELDS 8 TO 10 SERVINGS

Plenty of bacon plumps up the dried pinto beans that form the chunky backdrop for this fragrant and spicy version of traditional Boston baked beans. You can save time by using canned pinto beans, but you'll miss out on the toothsome texture. If you prefer, substitute dried kidney beans for a slightly different, but still very delicious, result.

BEANS

1 pound (450 g) dried pinto beans
1 medium onion, peeled and cut
   into eighths
3 cloves garlic, peeled
2 stalks celery, cut into 3-inch
   (7.6-cm) lengths
4 slices bacon
2 bay leaves
3/4 pound (340 g) smoked ham hock
2 teaspoons kosher or sea salt
1 teaspoon ground black pepper
Water

BAKING SAUCE

8 slices bacon, cut into small dice
1 onion, finely diced
3 cloves garlic, smashed and diced
1 tablespoon plus 1 teaspoon kosher
   or sea salt
1 teaspoon ground black pepper
1/2 cup (120 ml) white wine vinegar
1/2 cup (110 g) lightly packed light
   brown sugar
2 cups (475 ml) beef stock
1/2 cup (120 g) ketchup
1/3 cup (80 ml) real maple syrup
1/3 cup (80 ml) cognac or brandy
1/2 teaspoon ground cloves

BEANS The day before preparing, rinse the beans and place in a large bowl. Cover completely with fresh cold water 6 inches (15 cm) above the bean level. Cover and store at room temperature for 8–12 hours. Drain completely and rinse.

Place the beans in an 8-quart (8-l) ovenproof Dutch oven or soup pot with the onion, garlic, celery, bacon, bay leaves, ham hock, salt, pepper, and water to generously cover. Bring to a boil, reduce to a simmer, and cook, stirring frequently, for 1 hour and 15 minutes, until the beans have softened and are starting to break up. Drain in a colander. Remove ham hock and set aside. Remove and discard the bacon and most of the larger vegetable chunks. Return beans to the pot.

BAKING SAUCE Preheat oven to 325° F (160° C). Heat a large saucepan over medium heat. Add the bacon, onion, garlic, salt, and pepper. Cook until most of the fat has rendered off the bacon and the onions are softened, about 5 minutes. Add the remaining sauce ingredients and simmer together to combine and heat, about 5 minutes.

Cut the outer skin and fat off the ham hock and recover and dice any visible meat. Add the ham to the pot with the drained beans, stir in the sauce, cover, and bake for 2 1/2 hours, covered, stirring once every hour. If needed, stir in additional water. Mash lightly with a manual masher (Basic Mashing Tools, page 10) to break up the beans. Serve hot as a side to barbecue or baked chicken.

FRUITS, NUTS & BERRIES

In this chapter, we merge the regal colors and sweet tartness of fresh berries with sorbets, ice creams, crumbles, puddings, and compotes. Often layered with crushed cookies, such as the sumptuous Orange Curd and Blueberry Shortbread Parfaits (page 167), or meringue in Ruby-Red Pavlova and Cream (page 164), these desserts reach ethereal heights with minimum effort and showstopping presentations.

Making your own ice cream or sorbet is so easy to do and so much better than most commercial brands. While they can be made without a machine, buying one is such a small investment in relation to significant dividend yields, especially for huge ice cream fans. The trick is to remember to freeze the bowl the night before and get the ice cream really cold before actually freezing it with the help of the machine. Sorbet or ice cream can be frozen in a bowl in the freezer and broken up with a fork at 15-minute intervals until frozen, but the texture results are not nearly as smooth or creamy.

Classics like applesauce and banana bread get refreshingly simple new twists in Roasted Applesauce (page 174) and Date Line–Sour Cream Banana Bread (page 177); they are so simply delicious that I think you'll find yourself returning to these recipe pages again and again.

MINTY WATERMELON SORBET

YIELDS 1 QUART (1 L)

Sorbet is such a refreshing and surprisingly easy treat to make, especially with the fresh, sweet fruits of summer, when cool bowls of goodness are especially welcome. The sorbet is composed of a simple syrup (equal parts sugar and water) and smashed or puréed fresh fruit, and the trick is getting the ratio of sugar to fruit just right to ensure a supple, smooth texture. To test if the ratio is right, simply place a washed egg on its side on top of the cold sorbet base. If the egg stays afloat, showing about a nickel-size bit of shell above the base, you've got it. If not, the base needs more sugar. Remember, it's going to taste much less sweet once frozen.

Here, watermelon gets a bright kick from fresh mint that is steeped in the warm syrup mixture. Fresh basil would also be a refreshing herb alternative. Remove the sorbet from the freezer and let stand for 15 minutes before serving. Garnish with fresh sprigs of mint and a small wedge of watermelon.

1 cup (200 g) sugar
1 cup (240 ml) water
1/3 cup (15 g) fresh mint leaves
5 cups (770 g) 1-inch (2.5-cm) cubes seedless watermelon
Generous pinch of kosher or sea salt
2 tablespoons fresh lemon juice

Place the sugar and water in a medium saucepan with the fresh mint. Bring to a simmer over medium high and stir to dissolve the sugar, 2–3 minutes. Turn off heat and steep the mint in the syrup for 15 minutes.

Meanwhile, put the watermelon in the bowl of a food processor fitted with a metal blade and process until smooth and frothy, or mash in a large bowl to a fine pulp using a manual masher (Basic Mashing Tools, page 10). Pour the processed mixture into a large bowl, or using the same bowl for manually mashed watermelon, and add the steeped syrup, straining through a fine colander and pressing against the mint to release all flavor. Discard the mint. Add salt and lemon juice and stir to combine. Chill for at least 1 hour.

When fully chilled, place mixture in the frozen bowl of your ice cream maker and process according to manufacturer's directions, usually 20–25 minutes to freeze. Cover with plastic wrap and freeze until ready to serve. Homemade sorbets and ice creams are best served within a few days of preparation. Do not store for more than 2 weeks.

MANGO, PEACH, AND VANILLA BEAN SORBET

YIELDS 1 QUART (1 L)

Mango and fresh peaches play so perfectly together, both in vibrant orange-yellow color and sweet-tart flavor. Tiny dots of fresh vanilla seeds pop in each bite, making this a sorbet to make again and again, particularly when summer peaches are at their freshness peak. To peel a mango, cut off the outer skins with a paring knife, and cut the flesh away from the large inner seed, which needs to be discarded. It's the same series of steps with peaches, just on a smaller scale. Peel both over a bowl so that none of the sweet juices escape the sorbet or your mouth.

1 cup (200 g) sugar

1 cup (240 ml) water

1 fresh vanilla bean

2 cups (330 g) 1-inch (2.5-cm) cubes fresh mangoes (about 2 mangoes)

3 cups (310 g) 1-inch (2.5-cm) cubes peeled fresh peaches (about 4 peaches)

2 tablespoons fresh lemon juice

Generous pinch of kosher or sea salt

2 teaspoons dark rum (optional)

Combine the sugar and water in a medium saucepan. Cut off the ends of the vanilla bean, cut in half vertically, scrape out the seeds with a small paring knife, and place in the saucepan. Bring the mixture to a simmer over medium high, stirring to dissolve the sugar. Add the mangoes, peaches, lemon juice, salt, and rum. Cook for 1 minute. Remove from heat and steep together for 5 minutes.

Pulse the mixture in the bowl of a food processor until very smooth and frothy. You can leave a few chunks, if desired. Pour into a large bowl and chill, covered, for at least 1 hour to overnight. Freeze according to ice cream maker manufacturer's directions. Garnish each serving with a bit of fresh vanilla bean, if desired.

BLUES-BUSTING BLUEBERRY ICE CREAM

YIELDS 1¹/₂ QUARTS (1.5 L)

I'm reprising this four ingredient and regally-hued creamy blueberry ice cream from my first cookbook, *Southern Farmers Market Cookbook* (Gibbs Smith, 2009). It's one of my favorites for its eggless, creamy simplicity alone. Use only the freshest summer blueberries in this recipe and rinse them just before using, no sooner.

2¹/₂ cups (370 g) fresh blueberries
1 cup (200 g) sugar
Juice of 1 small lemon
3 cups (700 ml) full-fat cream

Purée the blueberries with the sugar and lemon juice in the bowl of a food processor fitted with a metal blade until smooth, or process with a manual masher (Basic Mashing Tools, page 10) in a bowl until chunky smooth. Whisk in the cream until thoroughly combined. Pour into an ice cream maker and freeze according to the manufacturer's directions. Serve in bowls garnished with a few fresh blueberries and a sprig of mint.

EXTRA CREAMY RASPBERRY ICE CREAM

YIELDS 1¹/₂ QUARTS (1.5 L)

The addition of egg yolks in a classic crème-anglaise custard-ice-cream base give this traditional ice cream a silky smooth texture and the mashed raspberries proffer a pretty pink blush. Appealing chunks of fruit float through the cream just begging for the next spoonful.

2 cups (145 g) fresh or frozen and thawed raspberries
2 cups (475 ml) half-and-half
1 cup (240 ml) full-fat cream
1 teaspoon real vanilla extract
4 egg yolks, room temperature
1 cup (200 g) sugar
Pinch of kosher or sea salt

Gently mash the berries with a manual masher (Basic Mashing Tools, page 10) in a medium bowl and set aside. Combine the half-and-half, cream, and vanilla in a medium saucepan. Bring to a simmer over medium-high heat.

Meanwhile, combine the egg yolks and sugar in a large bowl. Whisk until lemony colored and lightened, about 2 minutes. When the cream mixture is just simmering, stream into the egg yolks and sugar, whisking constantly until combined. Return the cream and egg mixture to the same saucepan. Cook, whisking constantly over medium-low heat, until the large bubbles on top disappear and the custard clings to the back of a wooden spoon.

Pour the mixture into a large bowl and stir in the mashed raspberries while still warm. Cover and chill, at least 2 hours or overnight. Pour into an ice cream maker and freeze according to the manufacturer's directions. Garnish with fresh raspberries to serve.

MASHED BANANAS FOSTER SUNDAES

YIELDS 8 SUNDAES

This classic brown sugar, butter, and rum sauce wrapped around flash-cooked and flambéed ripe bananas was created by Chef Paul Blangé at Brennan's restaurant in New Orleans in 1951. The dark brown sauce is just the right foil for the sweetness of bananas. Lightly mashed and served warm over commercial vanilla ice cream with a crumble of chopped walnuts, it is sublime and comes together in minutes. To flambé, carefully tip the sauté pan to meet your stovetop gas flame, or quickly hit with a lighter flame. The flambé is important to cook off the burn of the alcohol and increase flavor, although the rum can be omitted altogether. This is best served straight from the pan, but will store refrigerated and covered for a day or two. Reheat before serving over a few scoops of ice cream.

½ cup (1 stick / 115 g) unsalted butter, cut into 8 tablespoons

⅓ cup (75 g) lightly packed dark brown sugar

½ teaspoon ground nutmeg

¼ teaspoon ground allspice

½ teaspoon ground cinnamon

1 teaspoon real vanilla extract

⅛ teaspoon kosher or sea salt

4 ripe bananas, peeled, halved vertically, and halved again horizontally

⅓ cup (80 ml) dark rum (optional)

½ cup (60 g) coarsely chopped walnuts

1½ quarts (790 g) vanilla ice cream

In a large sauté pan, melt the butter over medium heat and add the brown sugar, nutmeg, allspice, cinnamon, vanilla, and salt. Cook together over medium-low heat, stirring, about 2 minutes. Carefully add the bananas and gently stir to coat, cooking for 3 minutes. Add the rum, stir to combine, and flambé, standing back to avoid the flame. Gently mash into large chunks with a manual masher (Basic Mashing Tools, page 10). Remove from heat and cool slightly for 1–2 minutes. Serve warm in individual bowls over 2 or 3 scoops of ice cream. Garnish with a tablespoon or so of chopped walnuts. Serve immediately.

DEEP-PURPLE CHERRY AND BLACKBERRY MILKSHAKES

YIELDS 2 CUPS COMPOTE; ENOUGH FOR 8 MILKSHAKES

Fresh sweet cherries and blackberries simmer together briefly with orange juice, vanilla seeds, and honey to form a luscious compote that would be delicious served over ice cream or yogurt, or, as it is here, blended with ice cream to create deep-purple, frothy, and irresistible milkshakes. Serve in tall glasses with straws and garnish with a fresh cherry and a few blackberries. The compote can be made a few days ahead, stored covered in the refrigerator, and blended at the last minute.

The shake recipe needs to be made in 2 batches to accommodate a standard blender size and will make 4 generous shakes. Repeat to use the entire compote recipe and create 8 shakes.

COMPOTE

1 cup (150 g) sweet cherries, pitted and halved

2¼ cups (340 g) fresh blackberries

1 fresh vanilla pod, halved vertically, seeds removed by scraping with a paring knife (discard pod)

½ cup (120 ml) fresh orange juice

½ teaspoon real vanilla extract

Pinch of kosher or sea salt

1 tablespoon honey

SHAKES

1 cup (175 g) cooled compote

½ cup (120 ml) whole milk

3 cups (400 g) vanilla ice cream

COMPOTE Place the cherries, blackberries, vanilla seeds, orange juice, vanilla, salt, and honey in a medium saucepan. Bring to a simmer over medium high, reduce to medium low, and cook for 20 minutes, uncovered, until the fruit has broken down into tender chunks. Mash briefly with a manual masher (Basic Mashing Tools, page 10). Pour into a bowl, cover, and refrigerate to cool for at least 1 hour or overnight.

SHAKES Prepare the shakes in 2 batches, placing the compote, milk, and ice cream in a blender (Basic Mashing Tools, page 10), and process until smooth and frothy. Serve immediately.

MASHED MCINTOSH APPLE AND GINGERSNAP-WALNUT CRISP

YIELDS 8 TO 10 SERVINGS

Sweet-tart McIntosh apples are coarsely mashed with fragrant spices, lemon, and brown sugar while they're still raw, which incorporates delicious layers of flavor and a delightful mashed texture lurking beneath the gingersnap and walnut crust. Delicious warm, room temperature, or even cold, this will become a favorite in your autumn baking repertoire.

5 McIntosh apples, peeled, cored, and cut into 1-inch (2.5-cm) chunks (about 6 cups / 750 g)

Juice of 1 lemon (about ¼ cup / 60 ml)

Generous pinch of kosher or sea salt

1 teaspoon real vanilla extract

1 tablespoon ground cinnamon

1 teaspoon ground ginger

½ teaspoon ground allspice

½ cup (110 g) lightly packed light brown sugar

3 tablespoons all-purpose flour

¼ cup (35 g) golden raisins

1 tablespoon unsalted butter

GINGERSNAP-WALNUT TOPPING

18 to 20 gingersnaps (about ½ pound / 230 g)

¾ cup (85 g) walnut pieces

4 tablespoons unsalted butter, room temperature

Preheat oven to 350° F (175° C). In a large bowl, combine the apples with the lemon juice and toss, coating immediately to prevent discoloration. Add the salt, vanilla, cinnamon, ginger, allspice, brown sugar, and flour; stir to combine. Mash with a manual masher (Basic Mashing Tools, page 10), pressing down firmly to break up the fruit into smaller chunks. Stir in the raisins. Butter a 1½-quart (1.5-l) ovenproof casserole dish with the butter. Pour apple mixture into the dish and spread with wooden spoon to level.

GINGERSNAP-WALNUT TOPPING In the bowl of a food processor fitted with a metal blade, process the gingersnaps, walnuts, and butter until fully incorporated and the consistency of sand. Spread over the apple mixture and level with a spoon. Bake, uncovered, for 25 minutes. Reduce the oven temperature to 325° F (160° C) and continue baking for another 25 minutes, or until the topping is golden brown and the apple juices are just beginning to bubble around the sides. Serve warm, room temperature, or cold. Store, covered, in the refrigerator for up to 3 days.

PANNA COTTA WITH ROASTED MEYER LEMON GLAZE AND FRESH BLUEBERRIES

YIELDS 8 SERVINGS

Panna cotta hails from Tuscany and is a pudding of cream and milk thickened with gelatin. Its mild, delicate base invites almost everything under the sun in terms of pairings. Since my sweet neighbor arrived at my doorstep bearing a bushel of freshly picked Meyer lemons (the darling of the citrus world for their delicate lemon-orange flavor and stunning aroma) while I was working on some panna cotta ideas for this book, I decided to roast them and turn them into a mashed compote glaze to finish the panna cotta. The sun-yellow color and citrus topping is a winner, especially when finished with fresh blueberries. The panna cotta can be made ahead, covered, and refrigerated for 2–3 days. Add the compote glaze just before serving.

MEYER LEMON GLAZE

4 large Meyer lemons or 2 navel oranges and 2 traditional lemons, ¼-inch (6-mm) of tops removed

4 (6- x 6-inch /15- x 15-cm) squares aluminum foil

½ cup (100 g) sugar

½ cup (75 g) fresh blueberries

MEYER LEMON GLAZE Preheat oven to 400° F (200° C). Tightly wrap the lemons in the aluminum foil and arrange on a baking sheet. Roast for 1 hour, or until soft. Remove from oven and cool until easily handled. Open up the tops of the foil packets and carefully pour the juices gathered in the bottom of the packets into a medium saucepan. Half the lemons and cut into 1-inch chunks, pulling out any seeds and central pith veins.

Place the fruit in the saucepan with the roasting juices. Add the sugar; bring to a simmer over medium heat and cook, uncovered, for 10 minutes. Pour into a colander over a medium bowl and mash firmly with a manual masher (Basic Mashing Tools, page 10). Discard the solids. Return the compote to the pan, stir in the blueberries, and cook for 10 minutes. This will yield about ¾ cup (175 g) of compote. Cover and chill in a small bowl until ready to use.

PANNA COTTA

1 cup (240 ml) whole milk

1 tablespoon (1 packet) plain gelatin

3 cups (700 ml) full-fat cream

1 tablespoon honey

4 tablespoons sugar

2 teaspoons real vanilla extract

1/4 teaspoon kosher or sea salt

1 teaspoon finely grated Meyer lemon or traditional lemon zest

1 tablespoon Meyer lemon or traditional lemon juice

PANNA COTTA Meanwhile, prepare the panna cotta base. Heat the milk in a large saucepan over medium heat. Add the gelatin, stir, and heat until the gelatin is completely dissolved. Add the cream, honey, sugar, vanilla, salt, zest, and juice. Simmer over medium low until the sugar has fully dissolved, about 5 minutes, stirring. Remove from heat and cool at room temperature for 15 minutes.

Pour into pretty wine glasses or clear ramekins or bowls. Refrigerate for at least 3 hours or overnight, covered, until fully set. Top each with 2 tablespoons of the chilled glaze and fresh blueberries. Serve cold.

RUBY-RED PAVLOVA AND CREAM

YIELDS 10 SERVINGS

Created for and named after ballerina great Anna Pavlova, this delicate meringue and berries-and-cream combination is justly reminiscent of the airy, feminine flutters and flights of a prima ballerina. Here, fresh strawberries are mashed and combined with pomegranate for regal aplomb. The berries can be spooned over whole meringue discs, or perhaps better yet, break up the meringues into large chunks (better for absorbing the fruits) and top with fresh whipped cream.

Meringue is not complicated, but take heed to keep all fat (including egg yolks) out of the mixing bowl. I like to wipe my glass bowl down with a paper towel and a tiny bit of vinegar to help remove any trace fat before beating the room-temperature egg whites. Keep all components (fruit mash, meringues, and whipped cream) separate and compile just before serving.

MERINGUES

6 egg whites, room temperature

1/2 teaspoon cream of tartar

1 tablespoon plus 1 teaspoon cornstarch

1 1/2 cups (300 g) sugar

1 teaspoon real vanilla extract

MERINGUES Preheat oven to 275° F (135° C). Place the egg whites and cream of tartar in a clean large glass bowl. Separately, combine the cornstarch and sugar in a small bowl. Using a hand mixer or stand mixer, wake up the egg whites and cream of tartar with a quick blend on low speed. Keep mixing, on medium high, until soft peaks start to form. Turn the mixer to high and gradually sprinkle in the cornstarch and sugar mixture. Keep mixing until stiff peaks have formed. Finish by beating in the vanilla.

Using about 2 tablespoons of meringue, drop 10 circles onto a baking sheet lined with parchment paper, leaving a 1/2-inch space between each circle. Using the back of the spoon, smooth out the top of the meringues, forming a small indentation in the center of each. Place in oven on center rack. Immediately reduce heat to 250° F (120° C). Bake for 2 hours, or until the meringues are light and crisp on the outside, and slightly chewy on the inside. Set aside to cool. The meringues can be made 1 day ahead, fully cooled, and stored in a tightly sealed container. Reheat in 250° F (120° C) oven to re-crisp, if needed.

BERRIES

1 pound (450 g) fresh strawberries, trimmed and halved

3 tablespoons powdered sugar

1 teaspoon fresh lemon juice

¼ cup (45 g) fresh pomegranate seeds (pomegranate arils, page 13)

WHIPPED CREAM

1 cup cold whipping cream

¼ cup (30 g) powdered sugar

1 teaspoon real vanilla extract

BERRIES Stir together the strawberries, powdered sugar, and lemon juice in a medium bowl. Macerate at room temperature for about 20 minutes, until the berries have softened. Mash with a manual masher (Basic Mashing Tools, page 10) until chunky smooth. Stir in the pomegranate seeds. Refrigerate, covered, for at least 1 hour and up to overnight.

WHIPPED CREAM Combine the cream, powdered sugar, and vanilla in a cold bowl. Using an electric mixer or whisk, whip until the cream is firm and has soft peaks. Cover and refrigerate for up to 3 hours.

To compile the Pavlovas, place (or crumble) a disc of meringue in a pretty glass bowl or wine glass. Top with ¼ cup (60 g) of the mashed strawberries and a generous dollop of whipped cream. Garnish with fresh mint, if desired. Serve immediately.

ORANGE CURD AND BLUEBERRY SHORTBREAD PARFAITS

YIELDS 6 SERVINGS

In this dessert, bright orange curd commingles deliciously with fresh blueberries between layers of crunchy crushed cookies, and it's all topped with whipped cream. And, it's deceptively easy to put together. Prepare the parts separately and compile just before serving.

ORANGE CURD

1 tablespoon finely grated orange zest

½ cup (120 ml) fresh orange juice

½ cup (100 g) sugar

2 large eggs, room temperature

Pinch of kosher or sea salt

8 tablespoons cold unsalted butter

BLUEBERRY MASH

2 cups (300 g) fresh or frozen and thawed blueberries

1 teaspoon fresh lemon juice

WHIPPED CREAM

½ cup (120 ml) cold whipping cream

3 tablespoons powdered sugar

½ teaspoon real vanilla extract

COOKIE CRUMBLE

1 cup (100 g) crushed shortbread cookies (about 10 Lorna Doone cookie squares)

ORANGE CURD Whisk the zest, juice, sugar, eggs, and salt in a medium heatproof glass bowl. Place over simmering water in a half-full medium saucepan, simmering over medium heat. Continue whisking the curd, constantly, until the froth on the top starts to disappear, about 10 minutes. The curd will start to thicken. Continue whisking, not allowing the bowl to actually touch the water, until the curd has thickened to a pudding-like consistency, about 20 minutes. Remove from heat. Whisk in the butter, 2 tablespoons at a time, until melted and incorporated. The curd will be frothy, light, and lovely. Cover and chill for up to 2 days before compiling the parfaits.

BLUEBERRY MASH Mash the berries and the lemon juice in a small bowl with a manual masher (Basic Mashing Tools, page 10) until chunky. Chill, covered, for up to 2 days before compiling the parfaits.

WHIPPED CREAM Combine the cream, powdered sugar, and vanilla in a medium bowl. Using a whisk or an electric mixer, beat until firm peaks form. Refrigerate, covered, for up to 3 hours.

To compile the parfaits, arrange 2 tablespoons of the crushed shortbread in the bottom of a pretty clear glass or ramekin for each serving. Top with ¼ cup (50 g) of the orange curd and then with 3 tablespoons of the crushed blueberries. Top each with the remaining curd (about 1 tablespoon per parfait), evenly distribute the remaining cookie crumble, and add a generous dollop of whipped cream. Refrigerate for up to 1 hour (not more) before serving.

RED WINE–POACHED PEAR AND RAISIN TART

YIELDS 8 SERVINGS

Meaty Bosc pears soak up the color and flavor of wine like thirsty, edible sponges. The addition of wine-plumped raisins in this gently mashed tart filling wrapped with store-bought puff pastry is hearty and delightful, just right for fall entertaining. Blue cheese and walnuts are folded in just before baking, adding to the fall mood and flavors. Remember to thaw the pastry overnight in the refrigerator according to package directions before compiling and baking the next day. Serve warm, fresh from the oven.

2 ripe Bosc pears, peeled, halved, and cored

1 1/4 cups (300 ml) Cabernet Sauvignon

2 star anise

1 fresh vanilla pod, halved vertically

1 teaspoon fresh lemon juice

1/2 cup (70 g) golden raisins

1/2 cup (70 g) crumbled blue cheese

1 sheet thawed puff pastry

Egg wash (1 egg yolk, splash of water, and pinch of salt blended together)

1/4 cup (60 g) coarsely chopped walnuts

Preheat oven to 400° F (200° C). In a medium saucepan, stir together the pears, wine, star anise, vanilla pod, lemon juice, and raisins. Bring to a simmer over medium-high heat. Reduce heat to medium low and cook, uncovered, for 10 minutes, until the pears start to soften. Break up the pears slightly with a wooden spoon and stir them down into the poaching liquid. Continue to cook, uncovered, for another 12 minutes, or until pears are soft and break apart easily and the wine has reduced to about 1/4 cup (60 ml).

Remove from heat. Remove and discard both star anise and vanilla pod. Smash with a manual masher (Basic Mashing Tools, page 10) until chunky smooth. Place into a medium bowl and refrigerate for at least 1 hour or, covered, overnight.

To finish the tart, arrange the thawed pastry on a baking sheet lined with parchment paper. Pour the chilled pear filling into the center, spreading evenly over the pastry, leaving a 1/2-inch (13-mm) pastry border. Brush this lightly with the egg wash. Top the pear filling with the walnuts. Bake for 25 minutes, or until the edges have puffed up around the filling and are golden brown. Remove from oven and cut into 8 squares. Serve warm as is or with a scoop of vanilla ice cream.

FRUITY AND NUTTY CARAMEL CANDY BALLS

YIELDS ABOUT 20 BALLS

Technically there isn't much mashing going on in this recipe, but these candy balls are so good that they just had to be included in the book. Salty, roasted, crushed nuts are folded into warm, buttery caramel with dried cranberries and raw pumpkin seeds and rolled into pretty little balls that are perfectly suited to finish any party or holiday celebration. Serve at room temperature. They will store, refrigerated and covered, for 3 days.

1 cup (200 g) sugar
3 tablespoons water
1/2 cup (120 ml) full-fat cream
1 teaspoon real vanilla extract
1 tablespoon unsalted butter
1 cup (130 g) salted macadamia nuts
1 cup (120 g) salted roasted
   pistachio nuts
1 cup (60 g) walnut halves
1/2 cup (80) dried cranberries
1/2 cup (65 g) sprouted raw
   pumpkin seeds

Combine the sugar and water in a small saucepan. Cook over medium-low heat, stirring 1–2 times, until the sugar is dissolved. Increase heat to medium high and cook for 5–6 minutes; swish the pan 4–5 times to help the process along. Do not stir until large bubbles form on top.

Continue cooking on medium high for another 5–6 minutes. The sugar will turn to caramel very quickly now. The bubbles on top become very small, the sugar starts to smell like caramel, and it very quickly turns a caramel color. When golden and fragrant, remove from heat. Carefully add the cream and vanilla (it will bubble up). Stir in the butter to finish. Return to stove and heat over low for 1 minute, stirring to combine.

In the bowl of a food processor fitted with a metal blade, pulse together the macadamia nuts, pistachio nuts, and walnuts 5–6 times until coarsely chopped. Pour into a large bowl with the warm caramel (be careful, it's hot stuff!) and stir to combine with the cranberries and pumpkin seeds. Pour onto a baking sheet, spread level, and refrigerate for at least 1 hour or overnight. Measure into 1 tablespoon portions and roll between palms to form small balls. Serve chilled or at room temperature on a serving platter.

PEANUT BUTTER-CHOCOLATE MILLION DOLLAR BARS

YIELDS 20 SERVINGS

A buttery peanut butter and sugar base is topped with a layer of chocolate ganache and crushed salted peanuts in these winning candy bars. Make the day ahead, refrigerate, and serve cold as the perfect finish to a dinner party or an after-school snack for the kids.

1 cup (260 g) smooth peanut butter

1/2 cup (1 stick / 115 g) unsalted butter, melted

1/2 cup (65) powdered sugar

3/4 cup (180 ml) hot milk

3/4 cup (130 g) bittersweet chocolate chips

Generous pinch of kosher or sea salt

1 teaspoon finely grated orange zest

3/4 cup (110 g) salted roasted peanuts

Whisk together the peanut butter, butter, and powdered sugar in a small bowl until smooth. Pour hot milk over the chocolate chips in another small bowl and whisk to combine.

To compile, spread the peanut butter mixture in an even layer in a 1.5-quart (1.5-l) square casserole dish. Top with the warm chocolate mixture and spread to level. Pulse the peanuts in the bowl of a food processor fitted with a metal blade until coarsely chopped, or mash aggressively with a manual masher (Basic Mashing Tools, page 10) to break into coarse chunks. Sprinkle evenly over the top of the chocolate. Refrigerate overnight, covered. Before serving, cut into small squares with a sharp knife. Serve cold.

ROASTED APPLESAUCE

YIELDS 2¹/₂ CUPS (610 G)

Roasting apples with a bit of lemon juice and sugar ensures that all of the juices, flavor, and nutrients stay in one delicious place, and it also yields apples so tender they are nary in need of a mashing. The McIntosh virtually melt on their own, while the slightly sturdier, sweet-tart Jonathan variety require a quick final manual mash. Perfect on its own, warm from the oven, this applesauce is lovely with a swirl of unsweetened cream, over yogurt or ice cream, or even as a side to roast pork.

2 Jonathan apples, peeled, quartered, and cored

3 McIntosh apples, peeled, quartered, and cored

Juice of ¹/₂ lemon (about 2 tablespoons)

2 tablespoons dark brown sugar

1 teaspoon ground cinnamon

¹/₈ teaspoon kosher or sea salt

1 teaspoon real vanilla extract

Preheat oven to 400° F (200° C). Toss all of the ingredients together on a rimmed baking sheet, coating evenly. Arrange in a single layer. Bake for 25 minutes, or until the apples are very soft and easily break to the touch. Remove from oven and let rest for 10 minutes.

While still warm, place the apples and all of their juices into a medium bowl. With a manual masher (Basic Mashing Tools, page 10), gently mash until the applesauce is chunky smooth. Serve warm or cold. Will store, refrigerated and covered, for several days.

DATE LINE–SOUR CREAM BANANA BREAD

YIELDS 3 MINI LOAVES OR 1 STANDARD LOAF

A central line of finely chopped dried dates placed between two layers of batter anointed with the moistness of sour cream and mashed ripe bananas is the inspiration for this exceptional quick bread's moniker. I prefer baking smaller loaves, as less bake time yields the most tender bread, but a single standard loaf pan will work just fine. A brown sugar–cinnamon topping adds another level of surprise crunch. Serve warm from the oven or toasted with butter for an extra-special brunch, breakfast, or dinner finish.

1 tablespoon lard or shortening

3 large ripe bananas (look for spotted but still firm)

1 large egg, beaten

1/2 cup (120 ml) full-fat sour cream

1 cup (220 g) lightly packed dark brown sugar

1 teaspoon real vanilla extract

1/2 teaspoon ground allspice

1/4 teaspoon kosher or sea salt

1 tablespoon vegetable oil

2 cups (240 g) all-purpose flour

1 teaspoon baking soda

1 teaspoon baking powder

1/2 cup (75 g) pitted and finely chopped dried dates

TOPPING

1/2 cup (110 g) lightly packed dark brown sugar

1/2 teaspoon ground cinnamon

Preheat oven to 350° F (175° C). Grease 3 mini loaf pans (each holds about 2 cups batter) or 1 standard loaf pan with lard. Set aside.

Mash the bananas with a manual masher (Basic Mashing Tools, page 10) in a large bowl until chunky smooth. Whisk in the egg, sour cream, brown sugar, vanilla, allspice, salt, and vegetable oil until fully combined. In a separate small bowl, sift together the flour, baking soda, and baking powder. Fold the flour mixture into the banana mixture in thirds, being careful not to overmix (this will make the bread tough). Fold until just combined.

Fill the baking pans halfway with the batter. Top with a layer of the chopped dates, distributing evenly. Top with the remaining batter. Combine the topping ingredients and sprinkle over the top.

Bake mini loaf pans for 45 minutes, or until a knife inserted in the center comes out clean. (A traditional loaf pan will take another 20–25 minutes.) Remove from oven and cool for 10 minutes. Run a paring knife along the sides of each loaf. Turn out gently. Cool on a wire rack for at least 10 minutes before cutting and serving. Cool completely, wrap tightly with plastic wrap, and store refrigerated. For maximum freshness, don't cut until ready to serve.

INDEX

Holly Herrick is a native of New England and cum laude graduate of Boston College (Journalism/Communications). She holds Le Grande Diplome (honors) in Pastry and Cuisine from Le Cordon Bleu, Paris, France. A multi-award winning food journalist, cooking instructor, and author of eight cookbooks, Herrick calls Charleston, SC, home, where she lives with her two cherished pets, chocolate cocker spaniel Tann Mann and Chutney Cat. Visit her blog and web site at www.hollyherrick.com.